UNDERSTANDING RETAIL

FOR CUSTOMER SERVICE ASSOCIATE

DR. N. V. R. NATHAN, SUMA M. A.

INDIA • SINGAPORE • MALAYSIA

Notion Press

No.8, 3rd Cross Street,
CIT Colony, Mylapore,
Chennai, Tamil Nadu – 600004

First Published by Notion Press 2021
Copyright © Dr. N. V. R. Nathan, Suma M. A. 2021
All Rights Reserved.

ISBN 978-1-63714-710-8

This book has been published with all efforts taken to make the material error-free after the consent of the authors. However, the authors and the publisher do not assume and hereby disclaim any liability to any party for any loss, damage, or disruption caused by errors or omissions, whether such errors or omissions result from negligence, accident, or any other cause.

While every effort has been made to avoid any mistake or omission, this publication is being sold on the condition and understanding that neither the authors nor the publishers or printers would be liable in any manner to any person by reason of any mistake or omission in this publication or for any action taken or omitted to be taken or advice rendered or accepted on the basis of this work. For any defect in printing or binding the publishers will be liable only to replace the defective copy by another copy of this work then available.

Contents

Foreword 7

Preface 9

1. **Introduction to Vocational Training** 11
   - 1.1 History of Vocational Training 11
   - 1.2 Salient Features of This Book 13
   - 1.3 Methodology 13
   - 1.4 Skill Requirement for a Trainer for Retail Programme 16
   - 1.5 Trainer the Change Agent 17
   - 1.6 Some Simple Guidelines That Can Be Followed 18
   - 1.7 Objectives and Learning Outcomes 20

2. **Orientation to Retail** 21
   - 2.1 Introduction 21
   - 2.2 Definition of Retail 22
   - 2.3 What is Store? 22
   - 2.4 Customer and Consumer 23
   - 2.5 What is Product and Service? 23
   - 2.6 What is Target Market? 24
   - 2.7 Who is Sales Representative in Retail? 24

3. **Evolution of Retail** 25
   - 3.1 What is Evolution? 25
   - 3.2 Evolution of Retailing In India 26

    3.3 Stages of Evolution 28
    3.4 Types of Retail 33

4. Retail Today 35
    4.1 Current Retail Scenario 35
    4.2 New Retail Definition 36
    4.3 Essential Components of Effective Retailing 37

5. Distribution Channel and Retail Formats 41
    5.1 Retail Distribution Channel 41
    5.2 Retail Formats 42

6. Inventory Management in Retail 47
    6.1 Introduction to Inventory 47
    6.2 What Is Inventory? 48
    6.3 Reasons for Keeping Inventory in Retail 49
    6.4 How to Manage Inventory in a Retail Store 50
    6.5 Role of Store Staff in Inventory Management to
          Maintain Optimum Level of Inventory 51

7. Store Teams and Store Daily Activities 55
    7.1 What Is Team? 55
    7.2 Nature of Work of Various Teams at Retail Store 57
    7.3 Store Daily Activities 60

8. Customer Service 65
    8.1 Customer Service 65
    8.2 The Importance of Customer 66
    8.3 Facts about Customers 66
    8.4 Good, Bad and Excellent Customer Service 67
    8.5 Complaint Handling 67
    8.6 Tips for Good Customer Service 68

9. Job Description of Sales Representative 69
   9.1 Principal Accountabilities of Saes Representative 69
   9.2 Ways to be Most Successful Sales Representative 69

10. Fashion Product Knowledge 83
   10.1 Men's Wear 83
   10.2 Women's Wear 91
   10.3 Kid's Wear 97

11. Food and Non-Food Products and It Placement 101
   11.1 Introduction 101
   11.2 Food Category 102
   11.3 Non-Food Category 108

12. Known and Unknown Loss Management 111
   12.1 Introduction 111
   12.2 Known Loss 111
   12.3 Unknown Loss 113

13. Staff and Customer Safety 115
   13.1 Introduction 115
   13.2 Food Hygiene 116
   13.3 Emergency Response Techniques (ERT) and
        Safe Working Practices 119

14. Selling Skills 123
   14.1 Introduction 123
   14.2 History of Selling the Tack Way 123
   14.3 Methods in Selling: 124
   14.4 Closing the Sale 136

15. Customer Relationship Management 137
   15.1 Introduction 137
   15.2 History of CRM 138

15.3 Consumer Behaviour & CRM 139
15.4 Role of Loyalty Card as a CRM Tool 141
15.5 Consumer Profiling 144
15.6 Popular Loyalty Programmes in India 146

Retailing Post Pandemic across the World *149*

Retail Terminology *157*

Annexures *187*

Foreword

When I went through the Trainers Handbook, I was extremely pleased to see the structure of the book, which clearly sets the expectation of the reader and goes about meeting the expectations of learning through simple words, pictures and examples. The book has been presented in a friendly way for the retailer as well as the retail associate. I am sure trainers in the retail business will find the book very handy to educate and develop retailers in the country.

All of us in the industry have to support such initiatives so that we are able to build the foundations of the retail industry on sound principles of retailing and customer service.

Although all of us know that inventory management is a critical to our business, all of us whether modern or traditional ignore it believing that after all it is in front of our eyes and we can cash it any time, but managing inventory to maximize sales and optimize cash is the toughest part.

Customer service has become a back office discussion point and not something that the retailer works toward delivering due to shortage of trained manpower. I am happy to see these issues being addressed in the trainer handbook.

Post COVID era retailing brings in a huge opportunity and a big challenge for the retail fraternity. Retailers who were used to sleeping during nights will have to be agile 24×7, because when they are sleeping the customer is shopping and their competition has kept the digital doors open. Secondly the retail associates have to have the ability to be up to date on the product features as well as have the ability to serve customers through digital means like end of aisle sale, whatsApp sale, video selling etc. This also creates a huge opportunity for women to get into retailing as many of these jobs can be done from home on an hourly basis not necessarily take up a full time job. I complement the authors for addressing the Post Covid scenarios for retailers and retail associates.

I would urge Dr. Nathan to translate this book into many languages, such that we are able to scale and reach good retail practices to millions of retailers in our country.

I wish Nathan & Suma.M A all the best for this endeavour.

– Mr. Nagesh Satyanarayana

Founder TRRAIN & Chairman Shoppers Stop Limited

Preface

India has often been called a nation of shopkeepers. Presumably, the reason for this is; that, a large number of retail enterprises exist in India. The retail sector is witnessing a transition from its traditional form to the modern malls, departmental stores, super markets, specialty stores etc. not only in metro and other major cities but even in smaller towns and taluka levels making the Indian consumers for a new shopping experience. It is rated as the fifth most attractive, emerging retail market in the world; India is viewed as a potential goldmine for global as well as domestic majors. With the strong economic boom, India's retail market is expected to cross $ 400 million by the end of 2011, turning India into the biggest market in the world. The reason for such a rapid change in the retail scenario is India's vast potential middle class and its untapped retail industry and the growing consciousness of the consumer about product quality and service. Presently, in the organized retail sector there is a huge manpower demand in terms of knowledge and skill.

In view of the large expansion in retail happening across the country, there is shortage of skilled manpower at the front end. This book would serve as a tool for structured self-learning, Training material for NGOs, Educational Institutions and vocational training centers who are making an attempt to develop skilled man power for the industry. The book intends to train Retail trainers in basic understanding of organized retail, store formats, store operations and teams, layouts and fixtures, customer service, selling skills, inventory management, customer relationship management, knowledge of food & non-food products and apparels. It can be used for an entry level program for students who are interested to start their career in retail as Customer Service Associate (CSA) and grow further with the industry.

– Dr. N. V. R. Nathan

– Suma M Appachu

Introduction to Vocational Training

 1.0. Objectives

After reading this unit, you should be able to know:

- The history of vocational training
- Background of the programme
- The uniqueness of the programme
- Methodology
- Skill requirement for a trainer for retail programme
- Trainer, the change agent
- Some simple guidelines that can be followed
- Objectives and learning outcomes

1.1 History of Vocational Training

Training has existed since the beginning of time itself. The ability to communicate a word or act to another being is an important part of human intelligence and has enabled the evolution of knowledge and understanding to its prominent position today. The earliest training was the transfer of survival information. This type of training continued as man and knowledge itself advanced.

Training developed into apprenticeships as society evolved. (This form of training still exists today in highly skilled jobs.) The apprentice, or the trainee, was assigned, or bound by contract, to a skilled master of the particular craft or art to be trained. The master taught the apprentice over a period of years until the craft or art was mastered. This was a good method of training skilled workers, but the industrial revolution soon made the apprenticeship program obsolete.

In the early 1800's, power driven machinery was invented on a large scale. Power driven machinery gave rise to the industrial revolution – the age of the machine. The small shop of the master craftsman gave way to the large factory. Requirements of skill and knowledge were reduced from the total ability to partial ability. Factories were built and villages and towns grew around them. Lifestyles and work habits changed.

The most common type of training still involved a teacher and the trainee and was centered on the job. This method is called on-the-job training. The trainee learned how to perform only part of the total manufacturing operation. Skills were developed on a smaller scale than with the apprenticeship was the primary training method until World War II. During this war, the training effort was organized so that a large number of trainees could be taught a job in a short time period. The vestibule method of training was developed to meet

this need. The vestibule method of training teaches the trainee how to perform the job before reaching the production floor. The trainee is trained to do the job and then put on a production assignment.

During the war, an English doctor, Dr. Seymour, studied the effect of training methods and sought improvements. Dr. Seymour's efforts led him to a scientific approach to the training effort that drastically reduced the learning time. Today's training methods are based on Dr. Seymour's basic system.

During its evolution, training has retained the same basic definition – to result in a skill or knowledge transfer from the teacher (instructor) to the student (trainee) so that the desired modification in behaviour results. That is training – a skill or knowledge transfer. You, as the instructor, must transfer your skills and knowledge to the trainee.

1.2 Salient Features of This Book

- Self-Learning tool
- Reference & guide book for a trainer
- Use of simple language
- Pictorial presentation
- Valid Indian Retail Examples
- Retail Terminologies

1.3 Methodology

The trainer should understand her/his job responsibilities clearly before conducting the course. The aim of the training course is to provide the trainees with the skills of handling future tasks in a store with high quality and efficiency.

The methods that a trainer should adopt for the implementation of an effective training course are listed as follows for reference:

For this the trainer is supported with an adequate support of strong class room content and Multi Media Based audio visual content and guidelines on subjecting the trainees through a structured methodology, which could broadly be categorized into

- Familiarization with Retail Evolution, its nature and its current scenario
- Customer orientation and their buying habits

- Familiarization with front end store operations and support teams
- Actual selling conditions and customer relations
- Introduction to the basic product knowledge
- Developing a right attitude to be the first contact person for the customers

The duty is to train the new trainee to become a qualified sales representative according to the planned training program. After analyzing the training needs of the trainees, the skills for them must be agreed with management on the skills inventory. (Skill Inventory is the set of selling skills and skill levels required by a retail store front end to achieve the desired output. We will discuss the skill inventory in detail as we discuss retail practices followed in a store)

1. Supervision

Give instruction, as required and supervise the progress of the training program to make sure the program runs smoothly. (We have an Audio Visual Content for introduction of different retail formats and their product lines, Sales Representative's role and responsibilities on the shop floor, relevant list of games etc. We will discuss it in detail how to evolve a session plan and Monitor it)

2. Hands on Training

The focus of the programme is on "Performing" and not just "Knowing". Lecturing will be restricted to the minimum necessary and the emphasis to be given to "hands on Training". The training method has to be individual centered to make each person a competent one. Opportunity for individual work is to be provided with the continuous feedback and corrections.

3. Programme

The trainer should plan for the course beforehand. If there is problem among the trainees, which may affect the training schedule, the trainer may need to adjust it accordingly. As earlier discussed a session plan may be evolved keeping in mind the local festivals and events, other conditions like staggering of power supply etc.

4. Job knowledge transfer

Educate trainees about the knowledge necessary for their jobs, which include retail environment, importance of customers, selling skills, understanding their responsibilities & team work, usage of retail terminologies etc. As far as possible try and keep the original terminology, or may be bilingual but always try to familiarize with the original terminology.

5. Record and report

To maintain an accurate and complete records of each trainee's progress at all stages of training for future analysis. We will evolve and discuss subsequently about devising formats and monitoring progress of the trainees.

6. Discipline

To develop the sense of punctuality in the trainees which would also be helpful for their careers ahead. To maintain discipline for market visits and in completing the exercises given during the class sessions. Educate trainees about the disciplined life and its benefits.

7. Planning

Planning the allocation of the trainees within each training session. Set the target for each trainee, and prepare a chart showing the potential output of each of trainees for their jobs.

1.4 Skill Requirement for a Trainer for Retail Programme

1. Selling skill

The trainer is as good as the trainees who learn from him/her. The trainer should have knowledge in the retail front end activities and should be familiar with each operation in the system. He/She should also have skills in all the related areas than selling on which the trainees are to be trained in the Training Programme. He/She must also have skills to answer the doubts raised by trainees in the class room and should be able to show the way out or an alternate way.

2. Experience and education level

It would be better if the trainer has the education of at least $10^{th}/12^{th}$ with 3 to 4 years of shop floor experience of the Retail Industry. Basic Knowledge of Computers, good hold on the local language and working knowledge of English. Experience in the field of training or leading a team is added on advantage.

3. Updated Knowledge about the Retail industry

The trainer should always keep his/her knowledge up-to-date by attending other training courses; seminars and events as trainee usually count on their trainer as their sources of new information. He should have knowledge of new retail ventures, retail process innovations, skill levels and skill sets required by different format of retail industry. (For e.g. a value retail format may require different type of skill set as compared to a lifestyle retail format)

4. Presentation skill

Training is an art of communication and so the trainer is required to have strong presentation and teaching skills. He/She may need to adjust his/her teaching methods in a flexible way for different students. As the target audience of this course is BPL students who are generally from a background that they have not had a chance to receive good quality of formal education, the language has to be very simple. It is also to be kept in mind that this is a skill imparting programme so the final outcome is to enable the Sales Representative to deal with the final consumer and sell. A good mix of presentation as well as demonstration skills will also be required.

5. Patience

Since trainees are often with very different background and experience, especially from BPL families their learning abilities are also varied. However there might be people with a good dexterity and coordination skills who will pick up skills faster than the others and should be provided requisite skills to fit into a sales representative's retail skill inventory.

6. Motivation

The trainer would need to motivate the trainee and raise their interests during the training program. One way to give the trainees more interest and satisfaction in their work is to make them understand the vital role that they play in their company. This could be coupled with role-plays and simulation exercises.

7. Communication

Keep people informed, since they will not feel part of something unless they have a good idea of what that something is and how it works. Make sure that they know how their job affects other people. Give praise where it is due; always say please and thank you.

1.5 Trainer the Change Agent

The Trainer is the most important part of this programme; this could be simply explained as follows. If you compare an industrial worker whose father was also an industrial worker, he might be aware of how industries work, what is industrial culture. He is familiar about industrial discipline; the concepts are not new or first hand.

Comparing this with somebody who is from an agrarian background or whose background does not have an industrial interface the concepts of industrial culture and discipline will only flow through the Trainer who is the entry point for the entrant to the industry. The Trainers will not only be an instrument of imparting skills but will also be medium for building the right kind of Industrial culture. This establishes the role of a trainer not only as a teacher but also as a complete mentor.

1.6 Some Simple Guidelines That Can Be Followed

All of us would have the fond memory of our teacher. We have appreciated our teachers for being our mentors and preparing us for our life. We are perhaps going through very difficult transitions that from being skilled people we are now into the task of creating skilled people.

The Best player in the team may not be the best captain or the best coach; he has to have the right mix of the subject skills as well as people skills. It would be worthwhile to take some time remembers our favorite teacher and write down why we liked our favorite teacher, and what is it that we liked about him. We have dealt with the role a Trainer has to follow. Now let us look at what could be some simple ways of being an effective trainers

Personal Touch:

It is always good to have some kind of a personal touch and know people personally, try to get the names of the trainees ask them to wear identity cards and try to remember their names. Call out attendance personally.

Content Knowledge:

It is important to have a thorough knowledge of the content you could rehearse the content, and practice exercises where you need to evolve greater confidence to be able to handle it.

Available Resources:

Make a list of all the available resources; keep some extra material ready always e.g. list of games, small class room exercises, role plays and extempore subjects for retail etc. Check what needs to be added, add whatever is possible. E.g. when you have a class for selling tricks, you can have a role play of two students, one playing the role of a customer and another as a sales person. Here you can analyze the level of understanding they have during classroom studies.

Maintaining Records:

It is seemingly one of the easiest exercises, at the same time it is one of the most neglected areas, we tend to rely on our memory even though we know it might not always assist us. The most important utility however would be analysis and trying to find out how our efforts can be more fruitful. Maintaining records of daily classroom activities, the exercises done in the classroom, a record of the hard copies of trainees' exercises and market visit experiences will make trainer analyze more for his training style.

Repetition:

As all of us are aware that this is a month long module and is highly structured we may still find ways and means of reinforcing concepts and skill. Also ensure that the demonstration and instructions are accurate and repeated in fairly the same way, to avoid confusion in the minds of the trainee.

Maintaining Academic Rigor:

The Programme primarily involves imparting of skill but at the same time being a structured programme should be made rigorous. Some pressure in terms of achievement of goals and target must be maintained. This will also mentally prepare the trainee to cope up with the pressure in the real Industry. Try to induce healthy competition.

1.7 Objectives and Learning Outcomes

The objective of the Sales Representative training is to provide basic knowledge on various formats of retailing that exist and how each are different from one another. The basic training will enable the trainee to understand and appreciate the role of the front end salesman and the responsibilities he/she would hold in meeting the customers need and satisfy the same by offering the right product and service by playing the role of a customer facilitator. Retail is all about detail, the customer from the time he/she enters the store to the time they make the final purchase depends on the ambience, product display and customer service provided by the facilitator. This training module captures the essence of retail and retail facilitation through the best practice managed by the industry and offers the learning process through a mix of learning tools.

2

Orientation to Retail

 2.0. Objectives

After reading this unit, you should be able to know:

- The meaning of Retail & Store
- What is Customer and Consumer?
- What is Product and Service?
- Target Market
- Who is a Customer Service Associate (Sales Representative) in Retail

2.1 Introduction

India has often been called a nation of shopkeepers. Presumably, the reason for this is; that, a large number of retail enterprises exist in India. In 2004, there were 12 million plus retailers compared to the 0.9 million in the USA. Out of the 12 million 98% are small family businesses, utilizing only household labour. Even among retail enterprises, which employ hired workers, a majority of them use less than three workers.

2.2 Definition of Retail

In the simplest terms retail is nothing but buying and selling. However, as defined by oxford dictionary retail means "sale of goods and services to the consumers". The word "Retailing" has also been defined in dictionary as "sale of goods to the public in small quantities".

2.3 What is Store?

The premise on which the retailing activity takes place is called a "Store". According to James Anderson, It is called a store for the simple reason that the Retailer keeps all essential goods in store until he finds a customer to buy. It

actually stores it until there is a need for the same by a customer.

Final customers make many unplanned purchases. In contrast, those who buy for resale or use in manufacturing are more systematic in their purchasing. Therefore, retailers need to place impulse items in high traffic locations, organize, store layout, trains sales people in suggestion, and place related items next to each other, to stimulate purchase. However, retail marketing remains the single biggest challenge for retailers today.

2.4 Customer and Consumer

Customer – Customer is a person who buys the product and service from an individual or an organisation to satisfy his need. The word derives from "custom," meaning "habit".

A customer is someone who frequented a particular shop, who made it a habit to purchase goods of the sort the shop sold there rather than elsewhere, and with whom the shopkeeper has to maintain a relationship to keep his or her "custom," meaning expected purchases in the future. The slogans "the customer is king" or "the customer is god" or "the customer is always right" indicate the importance of customers to businesses.

Consumer – Consumer is the one who uses the product. Customer purchases the product but not necessarily he uses the product. For an example, a servant buys breads from the shop for his master. In this case "servant" is the customer because he is making a purchase from the store and the "Master" is the consumer who is going to consume those breads. If in above example, the master himself goes and buys bread from the shop then he himself is both customer and consumer.

2.5 What is Product and Service?

Product – A product is physical, concrete, it can be weighed and measured.

Examples are bricks, computers, cars, gallons of syrup, etc.

Person who buys the product from the store is called "Customer".

Service – A service is intangible.

Examples are polishing the car, repairing the computer, laying the bricks, getting haircut done at saloon.

Person who buys service is called "Client".

2.6 What is Target Market?

A Target Market is a group of customers that the business has decided to aim to sell their products and/or services. One who purchases is a Target customer and one who uses it is a Final User. For example, Johnson baby products are meant for infants but it is not targeted at them. It is targeted at their mothers.

2.7 Who is Sales Representative in Retail?

Sales Representative is the pillar of the company. Sales Representative deals directly with the final customer. He is the first contact person for the customers, the first representative of the company. He gives various services to the customers as per the company standards and makes them feel comfortable shopping. He possesses very good knowledge of products, store, offers, promotions and company policies. A Sales Associate is responsible for maintaining outstanding customer service as per company standards, generating sales, merchandising, and safeguarding company assets.

3

Evolution of Retail

 3.0 Objectives

After reading this unit, you should be able to know:

- The meaning of Evolution
- Evolution of Retailing in India
- Stages of Evolution – Understand the Barter System, Rationing, Kiranas Stores, Canteen Distribution Stores, Janata Bazaars, Cooperative Stores and Modern Retail
- Types of Retail and the difference between Traditional and Modern retail

3.1 What is Evolution?

Evolution is the change in traits over the period of time. For an example, an evolution of human being from Chimpanzees to civilized man over the years and years. Evolution starts with the very basic of anything and adopts various changes over the period of time according to the environment and its demands.

3.2 Evolution of Retailing In India

Retailing dates back to the Bronze Age according to Paul Hermann. As early as 4000 B.C. the Arabs used to travel in caravans and traded at market centres in Mesopotamia and Egypt. The history traces that Indian traders sold their goods in the bazaar of Rome and Athens. The business transactions in those days were by barter system. The barter system means, "Exchange of goods for goods". People exchanged goods in small quantities for their weekly requirements on the shady day. They carried their surplus goods and exchanged it in small quantities for various things that they required for the household.

The dictionary meaning of Retail (sale of goods to consumers in small quantities) might have probably been pointing to this era. Over the years, from the Barter system to the time currency era came into effect, the retailing too has undergone tremendous changes. The traders in those days exploited customers for personal gains. In the period of ancient Greece, the traders were most despised community. Great men like Aristotle and Plato have condemned the exploitation of traders.

Trading at one point of time was considered as mean and despicable profession. However many centuries later the attitude of people changed because they realized that the seller added certain utilities like form, time, transportation, packing, preserving etc all of which required his skill, investment & aptitude.

Dwelling into history from 4000 B.C. it has been documented, as to how several countries had friendly ties and did trade with each other. Eventually all trade activities would end in exchange of goods and services. Therefore, from Vasco-da-Gama to that of British East India Company, each had the idea to explore and expand trade, exchange goods and services and to gain goodwill of the people.

All trade and commerce are economic activities. Therefore, economists have divided all the economic and industrial activities into three different groups. Namely, Primary activity, Secondary activity and Tertiary activity.

Under the Primary activities, we have Agriculture, Fishing and Forestry. The Secondary activities cover Manufacturing and Construction. The Tertiary activities here refer to services and distribution. Therefore, we may treat Retailing as a Tertiary activity, since it is part of services and distribution. Does this imply that retailing is not as important as the Primary or the Secondary activities? No, looking back into history, it was traditional that one country wanting to develop friendly ties with another actually sent an Ambassador to express its intentions of friendship. They usually carried expensive gifts and souvenirs that would represent the rich culture and tradition of their country. The friendly ties between the countries always began with exchange of gifts as goodwill; followed by opening up of trade between the countries, which have always been the Tertiary activity. Therefore, the importance of service and distribution from binding ties of trade relationship to the current day context of "good customer service" to develop goodwill and loyalty continue to remain as an important factor.

Looking from yet another angle also would prove Tertiary as an important activity. First, analyze the Primary activity like Agriculture, Fishing, and Forestry etc. Any agriculturist should ultimately rely on the Tertiary activities (service and distribution) to sell his produce. The Secondary activity like Manufacturing and Construction depends on services and distribution. Therefore, we may conclude that, service and distribution are important, and so is retailing, which falls under the Tertiary activity.

3.3 Stages of Evolution

- Barter System
- Rationing System
- Kirana stores
- Canteen distribution stores
- Janata Bazaars
- Cooperative stores
- Modern Retail

Barter System

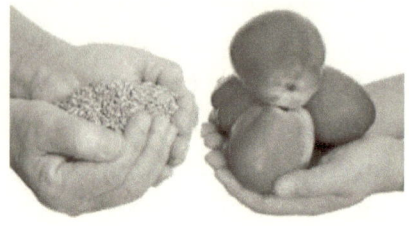

The earliest retailing activity commenced when trading activity started, in the form of Barter. Over the years, the currency came into existence, introduced as a negotiable instrument of exchange for goods and services. The importance and early stages of retailing is traced to the period when each town and village had a shandy day. Generally, the shandy day was once in a week and organised on the outskirts of

the village/town in an open area. People used to buy and sell goods during the shandy day. This marks the beginning of the first phase of retailing. This has been documented even as early as our Indus valley civilization. Retailing through entertainment like Walt

Disney has probably been inspired by our Sunday bazaar thousands of years ago, which had merry-go round, horse rides, elephant rides etc.

However, open market became a hassle during bad weather conditions and so tents were pitched to display goods and service, to be sold. Starting from pins, pearls to cats and cattle, everything was for sale on this shandy day in best of display to attract customers. As the level of earnings improved, the currency as a form of negotiable instrument came into existence. This brought in change in life style, the landlords set up the back yard barracks to store and sell small quantities even on a day-to-day basis. Commerce activity gave rise to a new community of traders. This enterprising community of small businessmen popularly known as the Vaishya community, set up stores to sell groceries, medicine, hardware etc. This was an improvised and reasonably organised activity and a full-time profession by itself.

Rationing System

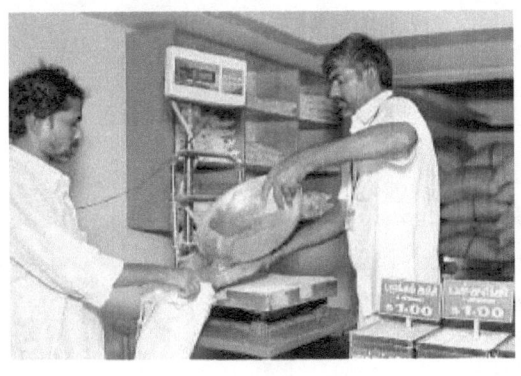

The year 1863 John Spencer and Charles Durant came to India and set up the "Durant & Spencer's" at Chennai. This set the trend in professionally managed organised modern retailing. At the same time India was going through the advent of Maharajas, who set up the treasury. These treasuries apart from having gold, silver etc. they also stored essential goods that were sent by rich landlords for favours to the King. The King in-turn used to distribute the items to the needy at a fair price. The British took over rule of India, ruled the country, and allowed the rationing system of essential commodities to loyal workers of the British Empire in 1939 beginning with

Bombay(Mumbai now).By 1946 over 771 cities/towns and villages were covered by the rationing system.

The Post-British era forced Government of India in 1949 to set-up a Public Distribution System (PDS) to distribute essential commodities like rice, wheat, sugar, kerosene, edible oil etc and averted famine in the country.

The PDS in the form of Fair Price Shops or Ration Depots is the earliest form of modern retailing the present generation can recall to the memory. This also happened to be the second phase in retailing.

Kirana Stores

The retailing also saw the small friendly neighbourhood Kirana shop (Provision Stores), which attempted to stock and sell virtually everything of day-to-day use. These small Provision Stores are the ones that satisfied the customers to the core. They offered oil for ten paisa and jaggery for five paisa at one stage to please the smallest of its customers. Kirana stores are owned and operated on a small scale, usually in a space of 500sq.ft. or less. These places are easily available within residential localities. Kirana stores are operated by the owners themselves.

Canteen Distribution Stores

The Canteen Distribution Stores (CDS) of the Indian Army has emerged as the earliest form of organized retailing selling over 30,000 SKU's and a case study by itself on logistics management.

Prof: S.Sadagopan, the Director of IIIT Bangalore in his article **"Supply Chain for Everyone"** in June 2000 has said "This single project of optimizing PDS in India alone would take the country to the "hall of fame" in the application of SCM; in turn it will be the most significant professional contribution leading to tangible and sustainable benefit to the millions of Indians".

The PDS caters to over 462,000 fair price shops reaching out to 160 million families across India making it the world's largest network in organized retailing. The PDS also is one of its kind examples of State-Central Government and Private enterprise partnership that has emerged as a case study.

Dr. Rob Jenkins of University of London and Anne Marie Goetz of Institute of Developmental Studies, University of Sussex jointly presented a paper in October 2002 titled "Civil Society Engagement and Public Distribution System, Lessons from the Rationing Kruthi Samithi in Mumbai."

Janata Bazars

In the year 1967, Janata Bazaar was opened in Mysore as the retail wing of MDCCWS (Mysore District Consumer Co-operative Wholesale Stores). Until then, the most sophisticated retail store was the neighbourhood Provision and General Stores. When the

first Janata Bazaar opened in 1967, there was excitement among shoppers, because it was planned as a "one stop shopping". From daily consumables to durables and textile of all hues and price points, Janata bazaar and its similar variants in other states of the country created interest in shopaholics.

Despite all the advantages, added to that the price being reasonable, being a part of a co-operative movement, this concept never took off. Reason was attributed as, primarily the customers missing that friendly, familiar chat and exchange of pleasantries that were experienced at the Kaka shop. Secondly, customer did not have the opportunity to bargain, which was a deep-rooted quality of consumerism in India. Finally, customers always had to rely on Mom and Pop Shop In the neibourhood when requirements were of smaller portions.

The Co-Operative Movement

Over the years, the concept of co-operative movement in retail remains a tale without a happy note; However Varghese Kurien changed the way Co-operatives worked. In 1967 he set-up the Gujarat Consumers Milk Marketing Federation (GCMMF) which created a history in International Co-operative movement. The brand "AMUL" went on to reach over 30 countries making it the only product from a co-operative movement to capture world market and today a Harvard Business School case study. Today, twenty-five years after GCMMF was planted as a sapling, much that AMUL has set out to achieve is a reality. It is a marketing success – recognized as outstanding achievements in Independent India and that too, achieved by a co-operative movement. This has come as a surprise to many in our country. In Varghese Kurien's words "While GCMMF is fulfilling its journey, it must never forget one thing – GCMMF work for the farmers and its future is indelibly linked to theirs. The producer was, is and will be the reason GCMMF exist."

Modern Retailing

The friendly neighbourhood Kaka shop or the grocer was the first level experience in shopping and customer relation. The Janata Bazaar and co-operative stores were the torchbearer of organized retailing and probably a little ahead in the conceptualisation. The present day retailing format has  traversed through a full circle by offering most superior features in ambience, quality, price and convenience.

Therefore, what we see today of Retail, is the "Re-tale of Retailing" like black and white classic movie remade in colour with special effects.  Spearheading the modern day retail revolution is Shoppers' Stop which in 1991 commenced operation and 1992 became the first large format multibrand retailer offering International ambience and best practice in retailing in India. Mr.B.S.Nagesh who was the architect of this revolution in retailing has been honoured in the "Hall of Fame" among the retail community of the world.

3.4 Types of Retail

The current retail has been divided mainly in to two categories.

1. Traditional
2. Modern

Modern retail – Modern retailing refers to organised trading activities undertaken by licensed retailers, that is, those who are registered for sales tax, income tax, etc.

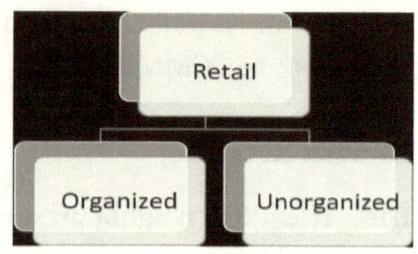

These include the corporate-backed hypermarkets and retail chains, and also the privately owned large retail businesses.

Traditional retail – Traditional retail refers to the unorganised formats of low-cost retailing, for example, the local kirana shops, owner manned general stores, paan/beedi shops, convenience stores, hand cart and pavement vendors, etc.

Difference between Traditional and Modern retail:

Sr.no	Modern Retail	Traditional Retail
1	Refers to Organised Retail structure	Refers to Un organised Retail structure
2	Company run business	Family run business
3	Many stores across the places	Only one store in own locality
4	Everything is fixed – salary of people, working hours, fixed item rates, fixed store processes etc	Everything depends on store owner's way of working
5	Big Bazaar, Star Bazaar, Reliance Mart, Shoppers' Stop, Bata, Pantaloon	Local kiranas shops, Owner-manned general stores, Chemists, Footwear shops, Apparel shops, Paan and Beedi shops, Hand-cart hawkers, pavement vendors, etc.

4
Retail Today

 4.0 Objectives

After reading this unit, you should be able to know:

- Current retail scenario
- New definition of retail
- Essential components of effective retailing

4.1 Current Retail Scenario

With the level of sophistication at which retail has reached today, the dictionary definition of "sale of goods and services to the consumers" has become insignificant, because retailing is no more just sale of goods to public in small quantities. Ask Shopper's Stop, Future Group, Westside, Food world or the Lifestyle Chain, They would say retailing is big and it's growing larger by the day. Retailing is the combination of activities involved in selling or renting consumer goods and services directly to ultimate consumers for their personal or household use. In addition to selling, retailing includes such diverse activities as, buying, advertising, data processing and maintaining inventory. With economy opening and the government favouring an open economy, more Global players are eyeing on huge opportunity of Indian retail sector.

4.2 New Retail Definition

With the changing scene, definition today for retailing should probably read as

> "Sale of quality goods and services to public at the right price, right place, right time, quantity and packing".

In today's cut throat competitive market, customers have many options to shop and satisfy their needs. Today's customer looks for the quality and worthiness in the products and services. The above definition emphasises main on four criteria namely price, place, time and packaging. In today's retail, it is very much important to meet these criteria at the right point. Below are some examples to clearly understand these criteria.

Right Price – It is very much important for a retailer to decide on the right price of his products according to the target customers, their preferences and lifestyle. A customer, who comes to Big Bazaar to buy clothes, will look for the clothes in mid price range and a customer, who comes to a branded showroom to buy clothes, will look for a high ranged and high quality clothes. Now, if the retailer sells the clothes above Rs. 1000 in Big Bazaar, he will lose his sales in clothes segment and in the same way if the retailer tags his clothes below Rs. 1000 in branded store, he may lose his customers due to suspicion in the quality of the clothes. So both the retailers have to price their clothes by keeping in mind their target market and its positioning.

Right Place – Right place refers to the perfect selection of the store location. The location of the store has to be selected by keeping in mind the catchment and target market. For an example, Big Bazaar targets the lower middle class and middle class for its products. So according to its target market, these classes generally travel by buses or public transport systems. Therefore Big Bazaar always built its stores near

Bus Stops on the main road only so that it doesn't become difficult for its customers to reach to the store or carry heavy bags after shopping. If the store is not at the right place, it may lose many of its customers due to inconvenience.

Right Time – Right time refers to the availability of the product when customer really needs it. Right time to sell the sweaters and warm jackets is from august to December because that is the time for winter season and customers need winter wear clothes in that period. In another example, if customer asks for Maggi noodles at the store and if it is not available at that time, it show bad replenishment and stock tracking practice of the retailer and customer may go to the competitor's store to satisfy his need.

This makes store location, product assortment, timings, store fixtures, sales personnel, delivery and other factors, very critical in drawing customers to the store. Let us understand the essential components for current retailing.

4.3 Essential Components of Effective Retailing

- **Service** – These days when customers have lots of options in the market, they choose one retailer who gives him better service than the other. These services include services like alteration, exchange, home delivery, gift wrapping, parking, baggage counter, well trained Sales Representatives etc.

- **Experience** – Experience refers to the look and feel of the store. Customers get attracted to the store by the unique shopping experience. This makes customer visit the store again and again. For an example, the Christmas decoration done at the store makes customers feel the festival and attracts them to come for the experience. Customers prefer experience stores compared to other stores for shopping.

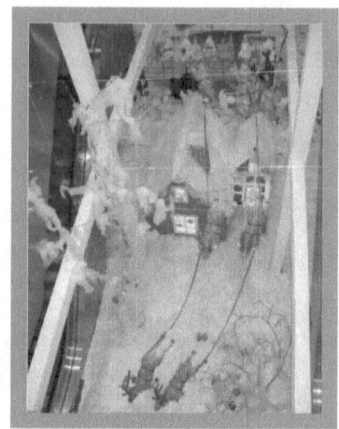

- **Product Assortment** – Selection of right kind of the products, at the right time is product assortment. Availability of the products which and when customers ask is very important.

- **Quality and packaging** – Today's customer is ready to pay more for a quality product. Packaging is the most attractive factor for the decision making. Packaging also attracts customers for impulse buying.

- **Variety** – Imagine yourself going to the restaurant for the dinner and waiter gives you just two options to eat or you go to buy a shirt for yourself in a store and a sales man shows just 5 shirts to you. Customer's don't prefer to go to the places where there are very less number of options available. That is why the concept of hyper markets and departmental stores works very well when it comes about variety.

- **Advertising** – In today's market when so many options for a single product is available in the market, it becomes very much important for a retailer to occupy the top of the mind position in customer's mind. Today when we think of noodles, we think of Maggi, when we think of a mobile, we think of Nokia. These products always come first in our mind due to its extensive advertising in the market.

- **Communities connect** – India has become a cosmopolitan country where all the communities live across the country. These communities are somehow connected with their traditions and habits. It becomes very much important for retailer to connect with these communities and do business with them. Connecting to the different communities and satisfying their unique requirements can bring more and more customers to the store. For an example, selling coconut oil in Delhi for a Keralian community or selling Khakhra to a Gujarati in south India.

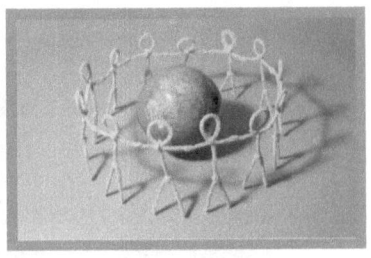

- **Store Fixtures** – Retailer has to decide on appropriate store fixtures according to the nature of the product. Generally shoe racks are transparent and slant because in such shelves customers can easily see both the bottom and front design of the shoe. For each product category, there has to be an appropriate fixture for comfortable browsing.

- **Sales Personnel** – Sales Personnel is the first representative of the store. They are the host for the customers who visit the store and make them feel comfortable shopping. Sales person can make and break the image of the company. Therefore, a retailer has to make sure to train his sales personnel for good customer service.

- **Store layouts** – In simple terms store layout refers to the placement of the products in the store for comfortable browsing. Which product should be placed in which area and near what other products is very important. A roll of toilet tissue paper beside a packet of Maggi is an example of bad store layout.

- **Best Deals** – A customer will always look for the best deal in the market. Retailer has to keep himself updated with the competitive market and offer the best deal at the best quality to the customers for repetitive visits.

- **Loyalty Programmes** – Loyalty means the trustworthiness. In retail loyalty cards are meant for the customers who visit the store frequently. Loyalty cards retain the customers by giving some extra benefits every time they shop.

5

Distribution Channel and Retail Formats

 5.0 Objectives

After reading this unit, you should be able to know:

- The retail distribution channel
- Different retail formats

5.1 Retail Distribution Channel

According to Philip Kotler, Retail is nothing but "breaking the bulk". Retail is the sale of products/goods or commodities in small quantities directly to consumers. Retail is the end point or nearest possible place, where the consumers find their required products. Retail sells to the consumer for direct consumption as there is no further marketing or selling activity continues after this retail point. Below is the distribution channel which shows the key links of retail supply chain.

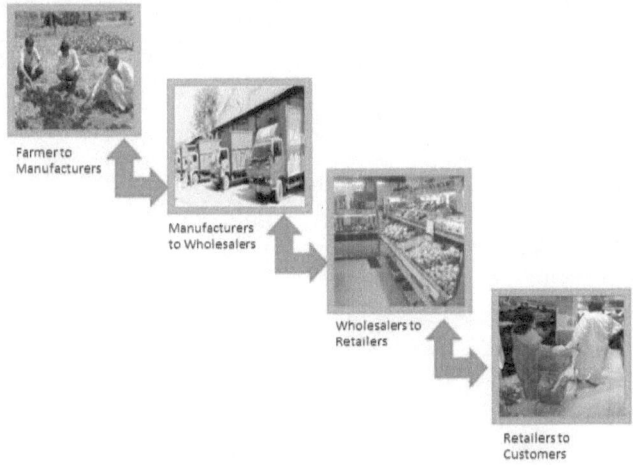

1. **Manufacturer** – Is the maker of the products/goods. Manufacturer owns factory to get the product made as per the requirement.

2. **Wholesaler** – Is the person who buys from manufacturer in huge quantities and then sells also in bulk quantities. He is also called trader or bulk buyer.

3. **Retailer** – Is the person who buys from manufacturer or wholesaler in smaller quantities and sells it to the consumer.

4. **Consumer** – A person who buys products or services for personal use. "A buyer of shirt is a shirt consumer."

Retailer has to deal with final customer so he has to spend on customer services, store fixtures, electricity, security and other related equipments. Retailer charges this additional money to the customers. That is why a same product is costlier at the retail store compared to the wholesale market.

5.2 Retail Formats

Retail stores operate in different formats. These formats can be classified according to the type of product sold, number of products sold, size of the store, speciality of the store etc. There are many retail formats. Some of them are listed below.

1. EBO (Exclusive Brand Outlet)
2. MBO (Multi Brand Outlet)
3. Kirana Stores (Mom and Pop Stores)
4. Category Killers
5. Malls
6. Department stores

7. Speciality stores
8. Discount stores
9. Hyper market/Super market
10. Vending machines
11. E-tailors

EBO (Exclusive Brand Outlet) – EBO refers to an exclusive brand store where all the available products are of the same brand. For an example, Levi's store. Here all the products right from jeans, T-shirts, caps, bags, shoes and all the other accessories are of Levi's brand only.

MBO (Multi Brand Outlet) – MBO is the store where many different brands are available under one roof only. For an example, Central, Shopper's stop, Lifestyle all are multi brand outlets.

Kirana Stores (Mom and pop stores) – Kirana, is a famous word in Hindi for this kind of store and in the west it is called Mom & Pop Store. It is a neighbourhood grocery store, a store which is in and around our homes/locality.

This is a format of retail which is majorly seen in India. This format is usually family run single stores which are seen in every part of the country and in every locality or area. These are our friendly, family stores where we shop for our regular food and grocery items and some small products for the house. This is usually a service store, where the store owner and his helpers stand across the table and give our requirement and help us.

Category Killers – Category killers are small specialty stores which have expanded to offer a full range of a particular category. They are called category killers as they specialize in their fields.

- Best Buy (Electronics)
- Staples (Stationary)
- Sapphire Toys (Toys)
- Sport Authority (Sports Equipment)

Malls – These are the largest form of retail formats. They provide an ideal shopping experience by providing a mix of all kinds of products and services, food and entertainment under one roof.

- Mantri Mall
- Garuda Mall

Department Stores – These are the general merchandise retailers offering various kinds of quality products and services. These do not offer full service category products and some carry a selective product line. Shopper's Stop, central are the best examples for department stores

Speciality stores – Speciality store is a retail chain, which deals in specific category and provides deep assortment in that particular category. Bata started one of the earliest specialty stores in India by

entering in to only footwear category and providing a wide range of footwear in its stores.

- Crossword
- Planet M

Discount stores – Stores with comparatively less price in the market are called discount stores like Big Bazaar, Star bazaar. These stores buy products in bulk quantity for lesser prices and sell it to the customer with fewer margins. These are the stores or factory outlets that provide discount on the MRP items. They focus on mass selling and reaching economies of scale or selling the stock left after the season is over.

There are discount stores called "Factory outlets". Fashion business runs mainly on two seasons namely Spring Summer and Autumn Winter. Stores which are in fashion business, have to launch new collection every 6 months with the change in season. So the old stock has to be replaced with the new stock. This old stock is being sent to the factory outlets of the brand and sold at the discount prices. Sometimes, fresh stock with minor defects which cannot be sold in the brand showroom is also being sent to the "Factory outlets".

Hypermarkets/Supermarkets: These are generally large self-service outlets, offering a variety of categories with deep assortments. They offer food, clothes, furniture, electronics, home needs etc.

- Big Bazaar
- Star Bazaar
- More

Vending – This kind of retailing is making incursions into the industry. Smaller products such as beverages, snacks are some of the items that can be bought through vending machines. These machines usually do not require any man power to sell the products. A customer has to put money or token inside the machine and a product will automatically come out from the machine. At present, it is not very common in India. Weighing machines and gaming equipment at malls in gaming zones are some of the examples of the vending machines in India.

E-tailers: Internet selling is becoming very much prevalent in the current retail market. These retailers provide online facility of buying and selling products and services. They provide a picture and description of the product, its price and benefits. A customer can buy product online by using his credit card number or net banking facility.

- Amazon.com
- Ebay.com

6

Inventory Management in Retail

 ## 6.1 Introduction to Inventory

During the initial years of retail evolution, there existed only few local retailers to cater the need of local people. Basic necessities like bread and eggs were being satisfied by a local grocery store and for garments; people either used to buy fabrics and get it tailored or buy what was available in the market. So buying for these retailers was a much simpler task. They didn't need to carry the huge stock to satisfy the limited and mostly predefined need. Number of suppliers were also very less and managing them was fairly simple and easy for retailers. Below is the basic supply chain which used to take place in early days.

However, as market expanded and the retailers' business grew; the number of products that were offered by the retailer also increased. While the number of suppliers increased, there was also an increased pressure on margins. Retailers needed to think of ways of cutting costs. In order to be able to cut down cost, it was necessary to integrate the complete supply chain. Below is the pictorial presentation of supply chain in today's world.

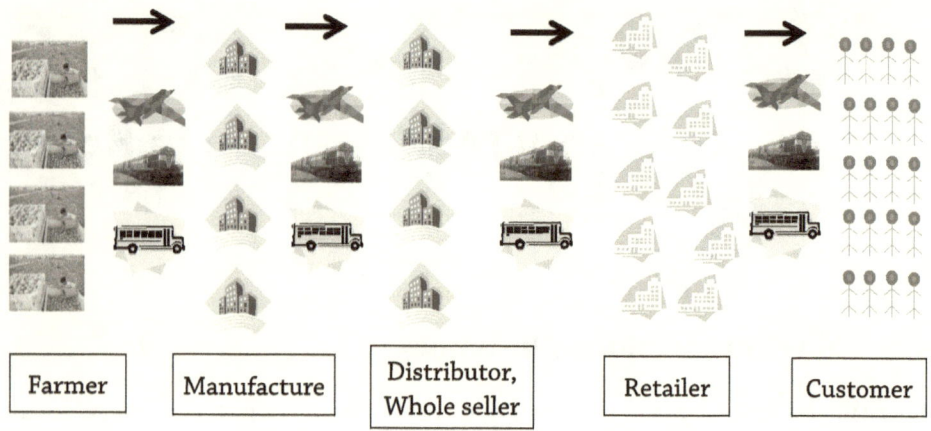

| Farmer | Manufacture | Distributor, Whole seller | Retailer | Customer |

Today, retailers operate in a dynamic world. Customer's buying habits are constantly changing, and competitors are continuously adding and improving their product offerings. Demand changes mean a shorter life cycle for the company's products and inventory. The cost of holding inventory may restrict the company from providing a reasonably priced product as funds are tied up in inventory. The number of suppliers to an organisation may vary from a few hundred to thousands, depending on the range of products offered to the customers. Sourcing, vendor management and logistic play a major role in getting the right product to the right place and at the right time. By looking at this changing retail scenario, inventory management is very much important.

6.2 What Is Inventory?

The word inventory simply means the goods and services that businesses hold in stock. In general, there are three types of inventories.

1. The first type of inventory is called raw materials and components. This usually consists of the essential items needed to create or make a finished product, such as fabric for clothes is a raw material. Fabric is not a finished product but it is a material that is going to be used for finished product called garment. Other examples of raw material or component can be

leather for a footwear or bag, wood for a bed, bricks and sand for a house.

2. The second type of inventory is called WIP, or Work In Progress inventory. This refers to items that are partially completed, but are not the entire finished product. They are on their way to becoming whole items. An example can be a cut fabric. A fabric which is in process to become a garment in the garment manufacturing factory is called Work In Progress inventory. In a same way, a house which is half built is also called Work In Progress Inventory because it is still not being finished and sold.

3. The third and most common form of inventory is called finished goods. These are the final products that are ready to be purchased by customers and consumers. Finished goods can range from cakes to furniture to vehicles. Most people think that only the finished good is an inventory but in actual situation, even the parts which are being used for making this finished product are also called inventory. In above example, garment is a finished product.

6.3 Reasons for Keeping Inventory in Retail

If we talk about Retail, the inventory is in the form of a finished product. Although holding inventory involves blocking of a firm's fund and cost of storage and handling, every business enterprise has to maintain a certain level of inventories to facilitate uninterrupted sell and smooth running of business. There are three main purposes or motives to hold inventory.

1. Time – It takes a good amount of time for a finished product to reach to the retailer. As shown in above supply chain figure, there are so many channels involved in the process of supplying a product from manufacture to the retailer. To meet with the

customer's expectation on time and to avoid the risk involved in time factor, retailers try to store some stock at their premises.

2. Uncertainty – Due to some level of uncertainty in demands of customers, sudden change in trend and other changing factors which affects consumer buying behavior, retailers have to maintain some buffer. Uncertainty also refers to the unanticipated problems at the end of supplier or transporter.

3. Economies of scale – In any business, two types of costs are involved. One cost is called fixed cost and another cost is called variable cost. In case of retailers, fixed cost is the rent which they pay for the store building while variable cost can be the cost which they use for the salary of their employees because it differs with the time. For an example, if the retailer is paying fixed cost of Rs. 1000 per month as a rent for the stock room and buys 500 units of products to store in that room, the cost per unit comes to Rs. 2 but when he store 800 units of products in the same stock room, cost per unit reduces to Rs. 1.25. This is called economies of scale. Thus, when more units of a good can be stored on a larger scale, yet with (on average) less input costs, economies of scale are achieved. So, bulk buying, movement and storing brings economies of scale in inventory.

6.4 How to Manage Inventory in a Retail Store

It is necessary for every management to give proper attention to inventory management. A proper planning for purchasing, handling, sourcing and accounting should form a part of inventory management. An efficient system of inventory management will determine what to purchase, how much to purchase, from where to purchase and where to store etc.

Retail inventory management is probably one of the most complex of all inventory management departments. In retail management, we have a greater variety of products to store and a great deal more of each product. In fact, the warehouse may never be big enough to hold all the merchandise that one need to keep in stock, and it can be difficult to maintain the right number of any particular item at any given time.

Retail inventory management should never be the job of a single individual but should be divided into departments and classified accordingly. For example, in a supermarket, you'll have two major departments – Food and Non-food – and each will have several subcategories. Under food, you can expect such departments as Ready to eat, dairy, Bakery, Beverages, frozen, fruits and vegetables and more. Depending on the size of your store, your retail inventory management could be divided into the two main categories and delegated to two individuals who would be responsible for the management of your entire inventory, or you could break it down further, having an employee in charge of each smaller division. This would allow the individual to gain an intimate knowledge of how quickly each product sold and how often it needed to be reordered. This would easily allow you to account for excess stock in some areas while others remained fairly empty.

The important thing to remember in retail inventory management is that you most likely have a little storage space for an enormous array of products and have to determine what will and won't be important to maintain in quantity. Being efficient in carefully stocking the storage areas, as well as knowing what your best sellers are, can help you keep your retail inventory management process strong and in balance.

6.5 Role of Store Staff in Inventory Management to Maintain Optimum Level of Inventory

Familiarise yourself with inventory management

As a department manager of any type of supply market, whether books, food, or any other kind of stocked items, it is necessary to understand the essentials of inventory management so that you can maintain a healthy supply of stock while not overtaxing your budget or storage space. When managing your inventory levels, you must have enough quantity, as well as variety, in order to please the customer. However, you must also take into account several factors that concern your position as the department manager.

Concern for Space

For example, your storage or warehousing space will greatly effect decisions you make regarding the amount of products and supplies you keep on hand at any given time. If you have extra space in your warehouse, you should analyze what products are the "best sellers", or the fastest moving items, so that you can wisely fill that space with these items. At the same time, you don't want to overstock on expensive or slow-moving items.

Movement of Product

Always look at how well your inventory moves prior to ordering. This is essential in inventory management in order to keep items from getting old while stored. This is especially important if you work with any kind of perishables. In fact, in these instances, you should never store large amounts; simply make sure that your supply chain can replenish your stock with frequency, and check your stock daily for anything that is no longer usable.

Cost Efficiency

Finally, be aware of the costs of shipping and receiving, as well as the total net worth of the items you have in your inventory. It is essential to document all incoming and outgoing stock so that, in an inventory check, all information is accurate. Whether you are in charge of a very small division or an entire company, you'll do well to understand the essentials of inventory management in order to profit rather than overextend the budget you're given.

The CSA can play a very active role in analyzing these through interaction with customer who always give feedback on comparative pricing. Inventory management is most critical to the growth of store and customer satisfaction and hence keeping tab on the inventory will help the store, inventory cost controls and also efficiency of the inventory management.

7

Store Teams and Store Daily Activities

 7.0 Objectives

After reading this unit, you should be able to know:

- What is a team? Retail Store Teams
- The nature of work of various teams at Retail Store
- What is SUSD (Shutter Up Shutter Down) and the store daily activities

7.1 What Is Team?

T.E.A.M. – Together Everyone Achieves More!

As shown in above statement, team has players that share common goals, a common vision and have some level of interdependence that requires both verbal and physical interaction. Teams come into existence through shared attitudes about a particular sport. They may come together for a number of different reasons, but their goals are same – to achieve peak performance and experience success. The ends may differ but the means by which one gets there is the same – teamwork. Every member of the team is accountable when it comes to teamwork. In retail sector, the goal is to satisfy all the current customers need and bring more and more customers to the store by giving excellent customer service, product assortment and shopping experience.

In Retail, teams are being divided mainly in to two parts as shown in figure.

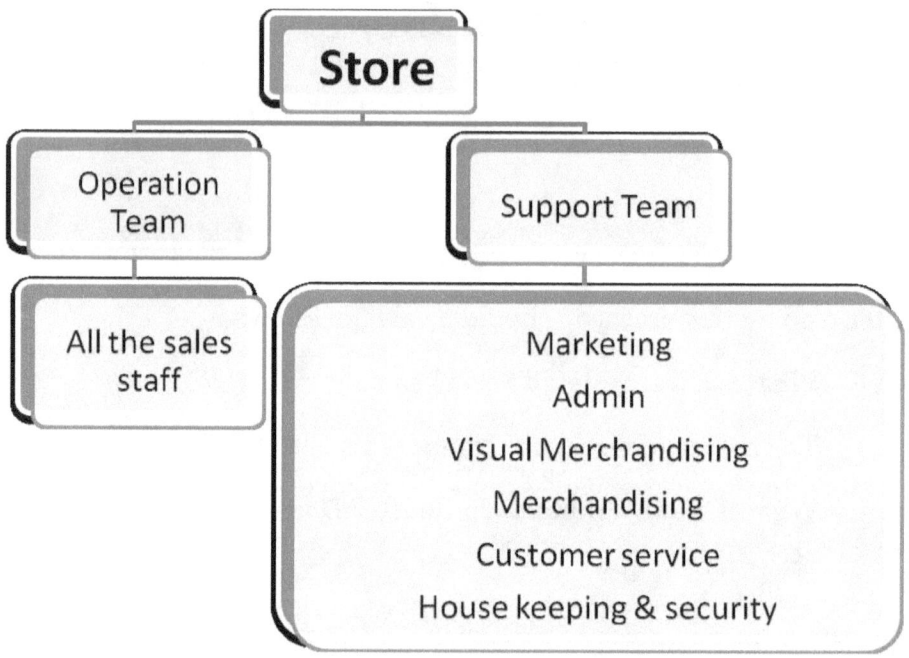

In retail, store teams have been divided in operations and support teams. These teams work together to achieve the best sale figures and increase their customer base. The operation teams focus mainly on sales. They set targets and deal directly with customers. It includes Sales Representative, Team Leaders, Department Managers, assistant store managers, store managers, operations manager etc.

While the support team supports the operation team to increase the sale by providing supports in the areas of administration, security, customer care, housekeeping, visual merchandising, HR, marketing etc. Let us understand the functions of each team in detail.

7.2 Nature of Work of Various Teams at Retail Store

Marketing (Brings Customers)

Marketing team's main function is to bring customers to the store. Marketing team is involved in collecting the customer data base, their choices, habits, lifestyle and other demographic and psychographic factors.

By analysing all these factors of the target customers in the catchment area of the store, marketing team comes up with appropriate promotional schemes. Their main function is to increase customer walk-ins in to the store. Marketing team also communicates the store benefits and promotions to the customers through News papers, flyers, hoardings, radio, TV ads, road shows and other promotional activities.

Visual Merchandising (In store Communication, Display)

As the name says, Visual Merchandising (VM) team works towards designing the visual appeal of the store. In simple words, the main function of the VM team is to make store visually attractive and appealing to the customers. VM team performs two main functions viz. communication inside the store and display of the merchandise. Whatever has been printed and pasted in the store for customer's information and knowledge is done by VM "Print and Production" team. For an example, directions, the store directory, pictures, branding, instructions, policies etc have been done by VM team as part of in store communication. In the picture shown here, the poster on wall communicates about some offer on Airtel Digital TV. This poster has been printed and pasted by VM team.

Apart from this, one more major function of VM team is to do merchandise display. The display varies from one merchandise to other according to its nature. For an example, formal shirts are always being folded and stacked while casual shirts should always be opened and hanged. VM team has to decide on which merchandise should be placed on which fixture and in what way. They also take care of colour blocking, size blocking, innovative display ideas, mannequin dressing, window displays etc. In the picture shown, the towels have been displayed innovatively on the upper most shelf to attract the attention of the customers. We can also see a very good colour blocking done in this picture.

Merchandising Team (What Merchandise and in how much quantity)

Merchandising team studies the shopping trend of a store and analyse the sale through of merchandise for that particular store. The job of a merchandiser is to order for appropriate merchandise for his store. He decides what merchandise to buy and in how much quantity.

This decision depends on the customer buying preferences in that particular store. For an example, a merchandiser in Delhi store purchases 200 pieces of formal stripe shirts and 50 pieces of formal check shirts while a merchandiser in Hyderabad store purchases 200 pieces of formal checks shirts and 50 pieces of formal stripe shirts. This happens because; in Delhi customers prefer stripe designs in compared to checks and vice versa in Hyderabad.

Customer Service Team

Customer Service Team is one of the most important team in the retail stores because they attend customers directly for any service required related to store or product. They guide customers for their queries related to store policies, they take care of the services like home 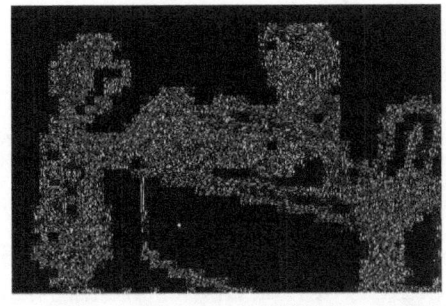 delivery, gift wrapping, alteration, lost and found, exchanges, issuing credit notes and gift vouchers, store announcements etc. Customer service team's main challenge is to handle customer complaints and resolve them by taking care of both company's policy and customer's satisfaction. In most of the hyper markets and department stores, customer service team has been provided a place called Customer Service Desk (CSD) in the store.

Administration team (Facilitates)

   Administration team is also known as facilitator's team. This team facilitates the store by supporting the activities like housekeeping, packers, loaders, maintenance, back office equipments and stationary, security etc.

Human Resource Team (Man management)

Human Resources (HR) team is mainly known for managing the man power of the store. The HR is involved in activities like manpower planning, recruitments, staffing, induction of new joinees, trainings, performance appraisals, promotions, transfers and demotions, retirement. Apart from these, they are also involved in developing employment related policies, welfare steps for employees, fun at work etc.

7.3 Store Daily Activities

We begin our day by getting up in the morning, doing daily activities during the day and ends with going to the bed. In a same way, retail activities starts before opening the store and ends after closing the store. These activities are known as SUSD in retail terminology which stands for "Shutter Up Shutter Down" activities. Retail activities are being divided in to three main types as below,

1. Pre-sale activities
2. During sell Activities
3. Post-sale activities

Pre-sale activities

Pre-sale activities are the activities which are done before opening the store in the morning. The objective behind these activities is to make store ready for customers to shop. Some of the pre-sale activities are as below.

- Cleaning the store – The store has to be cleaned before opening it for the customers. Cleaning the passages, sections, trial rooms, toilets, floor, shelves, products etc is must before

opening. The staff has to make sure if the carton boxes, trolleys and other packing material have been removed from the sales area and kept in the back room.

- Planogram followed – Following the planogram means arranging the merchandise in a standardised manner for comfortable browsing of the customers. Staff has to make sure the good arrangement of the  merchandise in his section before opening the store.

- Replenishment done – Replenishment refers to the refilling of the empty shelves. There has to be no empty fixture without merchandise in the store. Empty fixtures give wrong 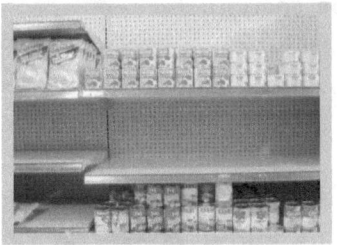 image to the customers about the merchandise and store. It also loses per square feet sale of that day. So it is very important for staff to replenish all the shelves and fill up every fixture with merchandise before opening the store.

- Display and signages – proper display of the merchandise and placement of the appropriate signages with its price and related offer has to be done before opening the store. These signages do basic level informative communication  with customers and allow the sales staff to focus more on sales.

- Price and security tags – A Sales Representative has to make sure to put all the price tags and security tags on the merchandise before presenting it to the customers.

- Location of bags, hangers, trolleys, and packaging material – Before customers enter in to the store, the facilitating equipments like trolleys, hangers, carrying bags etc has to placed at the fixed location of the store.

- Knowledge of store offers – It is very much important for the store staff to know all the offers running in to the store regardless their own section. For customers it is the whole store and not only one section. All the staff people have to study current promotions running in to the store before opening the store.

- Sales meeting – In every store, sales meeting is very important to know till date sales achievements and today's target. In these meetings, sales staff also discuss about the stock issues, customer preferences, missing merchandise and other matter related to sales and customers.

- Grooming – Before dealing with the customers, staff has to make himself presentable according to the company's standard. Grooming is very much important for the sales staff because they directly deal with the customers and represent the company's image.

During sale activities

Once store is opened, customers start entering in to the store for shopping. During the sale time it is very important for the store staff to make customers feel most comfortable in shopping and also to maintain the display throughout the day. Below are some points to take care during the day time.

- Welcoming the customers – Greeting the customers as soon as they enter in to the store.

- Guiding the customers – Store staff guides the customers for directions to various sections and to locate the desired merchandise in the store.

- Sales, Add on sales – Prime focus of sales staff during the day is sales and add on sales to achieve day's targets.

- Attending complaints – Attending and solving the customer complaints patiently and sustaining the store image. Store staff needs to be aware of company's policies for various processes at the store like exchange policy, guarantee policy, after sale services etc.

- Stock receipts and dispatches – During the day, sales man is also suppose to receive new stock from the warehouse. His job is to receive the stock and keep it in the back room and replenish whenever required. He is also suppose to enter the new stock data in to the system and do tagging for fresh stock.

- Replenishing and Refilling – During sales hours, it is very important to keep on tracking the stock movement. As soon as merchandise is out of stock on floor, the sales person has to refill it and get as much sell as possible from that merchandise.

Post sale activities

Post sale activities refer to the activities done at the time of closing the store and after closing the store. These activities mainly include the security audits and sealing the store. It includes below activities.

- Closing announcement – At the time of closing the store, customer service desk thanks customers for shopping with them and asks them to proceed for billing processes.

- Closing Audit – Security incharge does an audit for high valued merchandise. Stock counting for this merchandise is done every day. The merchandise is then being locked and sealed for safety reasons.

- Closing the cash counters – After closing the cash counter for the day, cashiers counts the money, collects all the credit card slips and submit it to the commercial department.

- Closing the store – After all the closing activities, a security person with one senior manager closes the store. The security locks the store and put a seal on it so that nobody can open the lock without permission from higher authority.

8

Customer Service

 8.0 Objectives

After reading this unit, you should be able to know:

- What s customer service
- The importance of customer
- Facts about customers
- Good, bad and excellent customer service
- Complain handling
- Tips for good customer service

8.1 Customer Service

Customer service is the provision of service to customers before, during and after a purchase. Customer service is a series of activities designed to enhance the level of customer satisfaction – that is, the feeling that a product or service has met the customer expectation.

Customer is the GUEST

G – Greet the customer

U – Understand customer needs

E – Explain features and benefits

S – Suggest additional items

T – Thank the customer

Customer is someone who comes to your organization for products or services – the end customer. These customers depend on the timelines, quality, and accuracy of your organization's work.

8.2 The Importance of Customer

- Customer is the most important person in any business
- Customer is not dependent on us. We are dependent on them
- Customer is not an interruption of our work, but the purpose of it
- Customer is part of our business – not an outsider to our business
- Customer does us a favour when they come in. We aren't doing them a favour by serving them
- A customer is not just money in the cash register. They are human beings with feelings and deserve to be treated with respect.
- Customer is a person who comes to us with their needs and wants. It is our job to satisfy them.
- Customers deserve the most courteous attention we can give them. They are the lifeblood of every business.

8.3 Facts about Customers

- The Customer is the business' biggest asset
- The Customer pays all our salaries wages and bonuses
- The customer will go where he/she receives the best attention
- There is no profit, no growth, no jobs without the customer
- A typical dissatisfied customer will tell 8-10 people about their problem.

- 7 out of 10 complaining customers will do business with you again if you resolve the complaint in their favor.
- If you resolve a complaint on the spot, 95% will do business again.

8.4 Good, Bad and Excellent Customer Service

Good service is when the customer gets treatment that meets his/her expectations. Bad Service is when customer gets treatment which is less than his/her expectations. When the customer gets a little more than what he/she expected, Good Service becomes Excellent Service.

8.5 Complaint Handling

Types of objections

- Lack of perceived value in the product or service
- Lack of perceived urgency in purchasing the offering
- Perception of inferiority to a competitor or in-house offering
- Internal political issue between parties/departments
- Lack of funds to purchase the offering
- Personal issue with the decision maker(s)
- Initiative with an external party
- Perception that "it's safer to do nothing"

If customer complains about something,

- Appreciate/Thank the customer for sharing the complaint
- Apologize for the error/mistake/inconvenience
- Listen actively and nod from time to time showing interest

- Show Empathy – Put yourself in the customer's place
- Resolve, if it is within your control. If not, bring it to the notice of your supervisors
- If not solved immediately, take down the customer's details (name, telephone number, address) to contact with the solution
- Do follow up till the customer is satisfied

REMEMBER: Don't take customers' complaints personally

8.6 Tips for Good Customer Service

1. Smile
2. Make yourself presentable/well groomed
3. Greet each customer as he/she enters your service area
4. Make an eye contact when speaking to customers
5. Be a good listener and show interest in what the customer is saying
6. Don't chat with other staff when customers are around
7. Identify & anticipate needs – Customers don't just buy products/service; they buy good feelings & solutions
8. Make customers feel important & appreciated
9. Avoid rushing or doing too many things at once
10. Apologize when something goes wrong
11. Service a little more than they expect
12. Use positive verbal & body language

9
Job Description of Sales Representative

 9.0 Objectives

After reading this unit, you should be able to know:
- The principal accountabilities of Sales Representative
- Ways to be most successful Sales Representative

9.1 Principal Accountabilities of Saes Representative

Regardless of industry, Sales Representatives play an important role in the success of their individual companies. Regardless of the type of product or service they sell, their primary duties are to interest buyers in their companies merchandise or services and to address customers' questions and concerns. Sales Representatives demonstrate their products and advise customers on how using these products can reduce costs and/or increase revenue.

9.2 Ways to be Most Successful Sales Representative

The primary responsibility of the Sales Representative is to offer friendly, helpful and expert service to the customers, resulting in the selling of merchandise, a positive customer experience and enhanced loyalty to the store.

1. Have a complete idea of the store layout

Layout is basically the floor plan of a store. A well-planned retail store layout allows a retailer to maximize the sales for each square foot of the allocated selling space within the store. Store layouts generally show the size and location of each department, any permanent structures, fixture locations and customer traffic patterns. Store layouts differ from store to store. Each floor plan and store layout will depend on the type of products sold, the building location and how much the business can afford to put into the overall store design.

- Straight Floor Plan

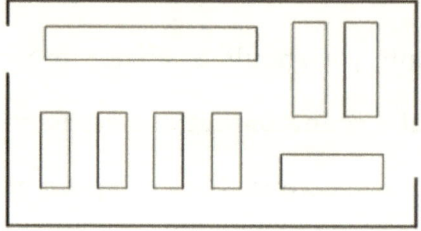

The straight floor plan is an excellent store layout for any type of retail store. It makes use of the walls and fixtures to create small spaces within the retail store. The straight floor plan is one of the most economical store designs.

- Diagonal Floor Plan

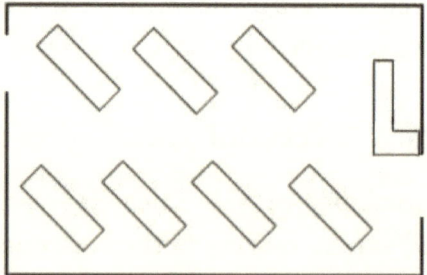

The diagonal floor plan is a good store layout for self-service types of retail stores. It offers excellent visibility for cashiers and customers. The diagonal floor plan invites movement and traffic flow to the retail store.

- Angular Floor Plan

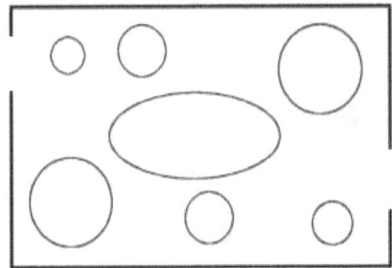

The angular floor plan is best used for high-end specialty stores. The curves and angles of fixtures and walls makes for a more expensive store design. However, the soft angles create better traffic flow throughout the retail store.

- Geometric Floor Plan

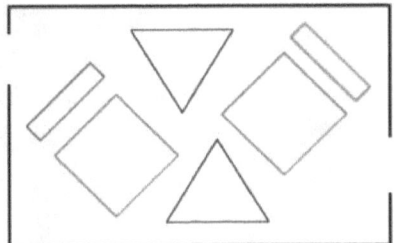

The geometric floor plan is a suitable store design for clothing and apparel shops. It uses racks and fixtures to create an interesting and out-of-the-ordinary type of store design without a high cost.

- Mixed Floor Plan

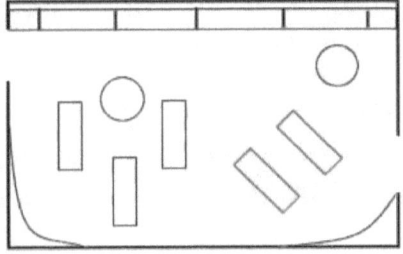

The mixed floor plan incorporates the straight, diagonal and angular floor plans to create the most functional store design. The layout moves traffic towards the walls and back of the store.

2. Understand the different categories and product

It is very important for any Sales Representative to understand all the product categories. This will help him to understand the customer's need and help them out by directing for the appropriate category and its location in the store.

3. Understand the store planogram and category adjacencies

A planogram is a diagram of fixtures and products that illustrates how and where retail products should be displayed, usually on a store shelf in order to increase customer purchases.

A planogram is often received before a product reaches a store, and is useful when a retailer wants multiple store displays to have the same look and feel. Often a consumer packaged goods manufacturer will release a new suggested planogram with their new product, to show how it relates to existing products in said category. Today, planograms are used in a variety of retail areas. A planogram defines which product is placed in which area of a shelving unit and with which quantity. The rules and theories for the creation of a planogram are set under the term of merchandising.

Planogram is primarily used in Retail sector. Fast-moving consumer goods organizations and supermarkets largely use text and box based planograms that optimize shelf space, inventory turns, and profit margins. Apparel brands and retailers are more focused on presentation and use pictorial planograms that illustrate "the look" and also identify each product.

Primary targets which should be achieved with planograms:

- creation of an optimal visual product placement
- creation of an optimal commercial product placement

In short, the primary targets can be summarized with a turnover and profit increase.

The visual product placement is supported from different theories:

- Horizontal product placement: To increase the concentration of a customer for a certain article, a multiple horizontal placement side by side of one product is applied. Different researchers found that a minimum placement range between 15–30 cm of one single product is necessary to achieve an increase in customer advertence (depending on the customer distance from the unit).
- Vertical product placement: A different stream with its follower is the vertical product placement. Here one product is placed on more than one shelf level to achieve 15–30 cm placement space.

- Block placement: products which have something in common are placed in a block (brands). This can be done side by side, on top of each other, centred, magnetized.

One can see the varieties of planogram results by simply visiting a local supermarket. Standing in front of say, a frozen pizza section featuring the products of a single manufacturer, one can see how the variety of products is displayed and how related products (such as pizza rolls) are treated in the overall product display for a particular pizza manufacturer. Similarly, one can visit the boxed cold cereal aisle, which comprises the various planogram strategies by the different cereal manufacturers. The ultimate effectiveness of the planogram of course is always measured by sales volume.

Next to the visual placement the commercial placement is the other important pillar of a planogram. Here the question has to be answered which products should be placed. Two factors for the decision-making process can be differentiated.

4. **Approach customers, greet customers and ascertain what each customer wants or needs.**

Recommend, select, and help locate or obtain merchandise based on customer needs and desires. Describe merchandise and explain use, operation, and care of merchandise to customers. Demonstrate use or operation of merchandise.

5. **Respond openly and objectively when attending to a range of customer queries and objections.**

6. **Bag or package purchases, and wrap gifts.**

7. **Close the sale**

8. **Maintaining the daily sales report and tracking the target vs. achievement**

9. Ability to up sell and cross sell

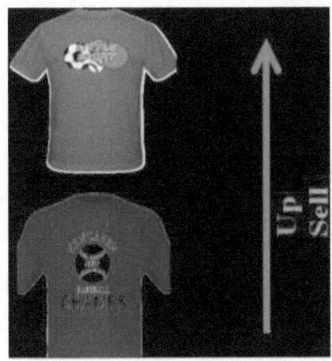

Up sell – Up sell is the ability to increase the bill value of the customer by selling him something more expensive than what he had asked for. A Sales Representative has to have good convincing skills, knowledge of related offers and very good knowledge of the product to justify its higher pricing. Beside picture represents one of the scenarios of upselling. If a customer is looking for a t-shirt within the range of Rs. 200, Sales Representative can try to sell him a bit more expensive t-shirt by describing its better fabric, good fitting and better design and thus increasing the sale value to Rs. 350.

Cross Sell – Cross selling is the ability to increase the bill value of the customer by selling him the best related product with the product he had asked for. A Sales Representative has to identify the hidden need, has to have good convincing skills and knowledge of best related products. Picture represents one of the scenarios of cross selling. If a customer is looking for a t-shirt, Sales Representative can try to sell him matching track pant. A Sales Representative can ask customer to atleast try the combination of that t-shirt and track pant and appreciate the same. Sales Representative has to have very good convincing skills to sell related products. If customer agrees to buy the track pant, Sales Representative can again go further selling him some low priced related products like a cap worth Rs. 50 or sports socks worth Rs. 100 and so on. Cross selling always helps Sales Representative to increase the bill value and develop good relation with the customer.

10. Recognizing the latent/future need of the customers and increasing their ticket size
11. Collect customer information, feedback, and data on customer buying behaviour, as and when required.
12. Understanding customer body language while buying
13. Everyday carrying global counting of stock in their section
14. Check and report any missing item to the manager immediately
15. Quarterly stock take with the scanners and dealing with the shrinkages
16. Displaying the merchandise in the most attractive way in the section
17. Mannequin Handling in the section
18. Making sure that all signage and shelf talkers are in place
19. Having a complete product knowledge
20. Knowledge of store equipments

RFID (Radio Frequency Identification) – The term RFID is used to describe various technologies that use radio waves to automatically identify people or objects. RFID tags are tiny microchips – about the size of a full stop on your computer screen – that hold a unique identifier number. They are attached to a small antenna.

RFID System Components:

1. Chip: will include memory and some form of processing capability.
2. Reader: read the radio frequency and identify tags.

3. Antenna: provides the means for the integrated circuit to transmit its information to the reader.

Some RFID readers

Security Tags – Security tags are technological method for preventing shoplifting/shrinkage/pilferage from retail stores. Special tags are fixed to merchandise or books. These tags are removed or deactivated by the clerks when the item is properly bought or checked out. At the exits of the store, a detection system sounds an alarm or otherwise alerts the staff when it senses active tags. For high-value goods that are to be manipulated by the patrons, wired alarm clips may be used instead of tags. There are two types of tags generally used in a retail store. One is hard tag and one is soft tag as below.

Hard Tags

Soft Tag

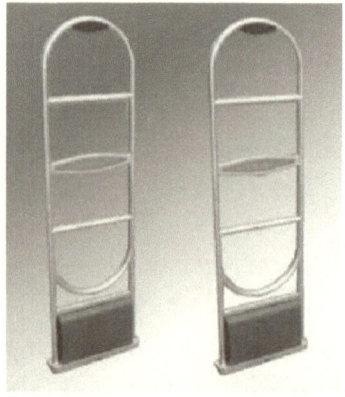
Detection System of tags at the Entry and Exits

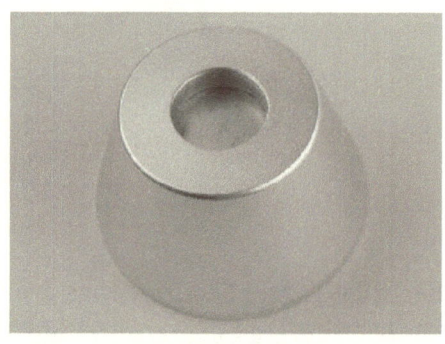
Hard Tag Remover

Retail Bill printers – In small enterprises, billing is usually done manually, and a lot of time is wasted – customers are often kept waiting. With the changing environment and Retail boom, business management of the outlet becomes the need of the hour. Receipt printers come in many variations and with many different capabilities. They have a wide range of connection methods as well including

parallel, serial and USB, which make it possible to have both a receipt printer and a system printer on the same computer. These printers work without fail forever. These printers require 3 inch wide paper roll. It will print in both black for positive and red for negative numbers and automatically cut the paper.

Cash drawers – A cash drawer is generally a compartment underneath a cash register in which the cash from transactions is kept. The drawer typically contains a removable till. The till is usually divided into compartments used to store each denomination of bank notes and coins separately to make counting easier. The removable till allows moneys to be removed from the sales floor to a more secure location for counting and creating bank deposits.

Barcode Reader – A barcode reader (or barcode scanner) is an electronic device for reading printed barcodes. Like a flatbed scanner, it consists of a light source, a lens and a light sensor translating optical impulses into electrical ones. Additionally, nearly all barcode readers contain decoder circuitry analyzing the barcode's image data provided by the sensor and sending the barcode's content to the scanner's output port. There are three types of scanners generally used in retail viz. dome scanner, hand scanner and bed scanner.

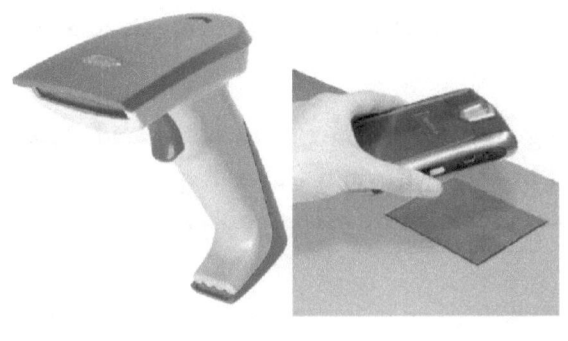

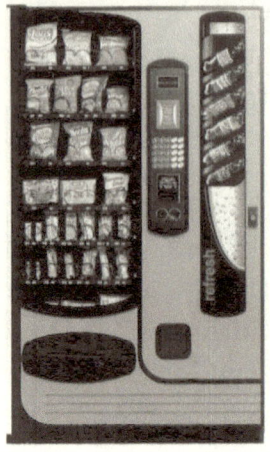

Vending Machine – A vending machine is a machine which dispenses items such as snacks, beverages, alcohol, cigarettes, lottery tickets, consumer products and even gold and gems to customers automatically, after the customer inserts currency or credit into the machine.

ERP (Enterprise resource planning) – Integrates internal and external management information across an entire organization, embracing finance/accounting, manufacturing, sales and service, CRM, etc. ERP systems automate this activity with a software application. Its purpose is to facilitate the flow of information between all business functions inside the boundaries of the organization and manage the connections to outside stakeholders.

Trolleys – A shopping cart (trolley, carriage, buggy) is a cart supplied by a shop, especially supermarkets, for use by customers inside the shop for transport of merchandise to the check-out counter during shopping. Customers can then also use the cart to transport their purchased goods to their cars.

21. **Knowledge of the store procedures and policies like Billing Procedures, Frisking Procedures, Alteration Procedures, Security Practices, Communication channels, Customer Services, Return Policies, Exchange Policies, Guarantee Policies**

22. **Remembering the regular customer's names and their choices of products. This will allow a Sales Representative to give personalized service and develop good relationships**

23. Advising customers about better products and encouraging them to buy and to return to buy in the future

24. Works with others as part of a team by supporting co-workers during busy trading periods so that ongoing customer service is maintained.

25. Ability to appreciate & willingly follow company's rules and regulations

26. Always stands for what will protect company's interest

27. Have a good attendance and punctuality record

28. Follow instructions and orders of the superiors in order to progress the work

10
Fashion Product Knowledge

 10.0 Objectives

After reading this unit, you should be able to know:

- Men's wear category and variety of products in it
- Women's wear category and variety of products in it
- Kids' wear (Girl's, Boy's and Infants) category and variety of products in it

10.1 Men's Wear

The men of this era are fashion conscious. There are different types of men's wear like Indian and Western, formal and casual. The Indian market provides a wide range of men's wear that caters to variant occasions and moods. Men's wear in India could be divided into two distinct groups – Indian wear and Western wear. While Indian wear made rapid progress through the business community and ethnic wear got added to it, the formal side got further sub-divided into formal suits and casual wear. Below figure shows the division of men's wear category in various designs.

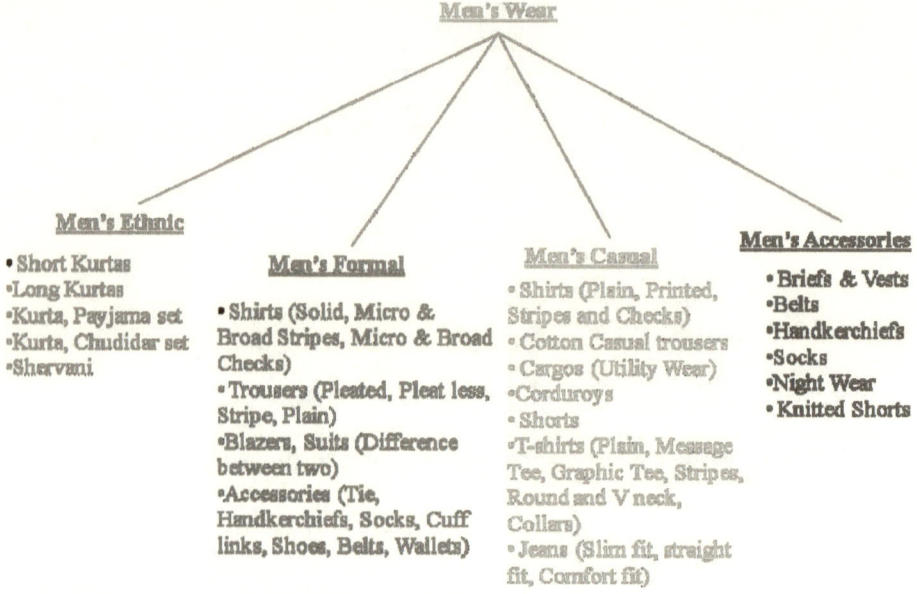

Men's Ethnic Wear

With the revival of a renewed interest in the grandeur of the bygone eras and a search for one's roots the attention is focused on high fashion Indian wear. Resplendent with the splendour and style of the ancient Maharajas and Mughal emperors, India's rich sartorial heritage has not only moved to centre stage but has at times even swept the west off its fashionable feet by its sheer majesty. The Sherwani, the Prince or Jodhpuri Coat, the Budni or Nehru Jacket as well as the Kurta Churidar have all returned to the forefront of fashion. Today western wear competes fiercely with Indian wear as the country's ancient culture and fashion has gained momentum. The Sherwani is the most traditional of Indian garments. Its extra long length of 110 centimeters and its

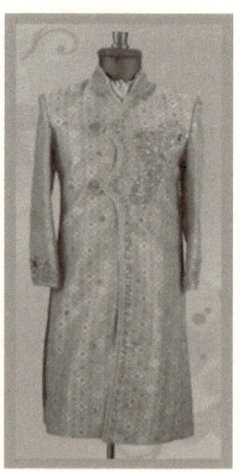

Shervani

Kurta, Chudidar set

structured body makes it a streamlined garment. The collar band is 3-4 centimeters. The colours are muted to dark and fabrics could range from broacade to terry wool. The Sherwani is normally teamed with Churidars or Aligarh pants which are a combination of Churidars and trousers. Another version of the Sherwani is double breasted or with an asymmetrical opening. Two inseam pockets and giant side slits of 25-35 centimeters are a must in the garment.

For casual lounging the Indian male's first preference is the Kurta/Churidar combination in light weight cotton, mills, pure silk or polyesters. The Kurta or shirt is either collarless or with a plain band.

The body of the garment could either have the 2-piece of 6-piece cut. Modern versions could be with a draped effect too. The Churidar or Indian pant is cut on the cross and has an extra length so that when worn it will crease at the ankles. The Kurta and Churidar both are in muted colours with delicate tonal embroidery around the neck and placket of the Kurta.

Short Kurtas

Long Kurta
Kurta, Pyjama set

The Bundi or Bundgala is the traditional long the Indian version or a western waistcoat that adds instant style to an otherwise informal Kurta Churidar. Fabrics preferred are raw silks, cotton, linen, silk, terry cotton, terry wool or brocade and for the sultry Indian weather the Bundi is the answer to formal wear.

Men's Formal Wear

Formal wear as the name itself signifies are worn for formal occasion like going to work, going for meetings or to official business related work. Some of the most popular men's wear brands in India are Van Heusen, Louis Philippe, Arrow, Peter England, Excalibur, Austin Reed, Lombard, John Players, Zodiac, Park Avenue, Vettorio Fratini, wills lifestyle and esprit. The formal wear is generally available in Solid Colours (Plain Shirts), Pin Stripes, bold stripes and sometimes in micro checks.

The fastest selling western garments are the shirt, trouser and suit to a certain extent. The shirt market attracts the most manufacturers who work for a large chunk of the estimated Rs. 500 crore business. There are nearly 5000 shirts manufacturers with branded or unbranded garments.

Micro stripes

Solid colour

Broad stripes

Micro Checks

Broad Checks

The formal wear market has consolidated and new segments of formal wear in trousers have begun to emerge as winners. The trouser which was the obvious follow on the readymade shirts has its own exclusive manufacturers like Zapata and Pantaloon. Every major shirt manufacturer prefer to team trousers with the garment to give a more coordinated look. The western suit and tuxedo are also a part of the men's wear scene and though they are available off the peg with manufacturers like Park Avenue and boutiques, the Indian male prefers to more often than not custom tailor them. Most department stores have a separate men's wear section that caters to the discriminating dresser.

Pleated trouser

Formal trouser (flat front)

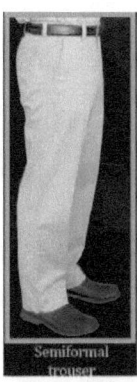

Semiformal trouser

2 pc Suits

Blazer

3 pc Suit

Below is men's formal accessory. It includes Ties, Cuff links, Formal belt, handkerchief, formal shoes, wallet and formal socks.

Men's Casual Wear

Men's casual wear is being divided mainly in to shirts, casual trousers, denims and T-shirts.

Casual Shirts

Solid shirt

Checks Shirt

Stripe Shirt

Printed Shirt

Casual Bottoms – casual bottoms include cotton trousers, cargos, corduroys, jeans, shorts as below.

Jeans

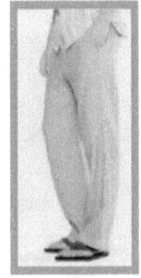
Cotton Trouser

Corduroy Trouser

Shorts

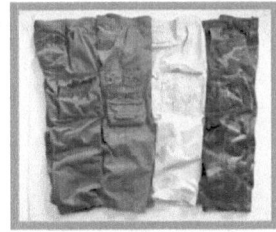
Cargos

Casual T-shirts – Casual T-shirts include various designs in cuts, sleeves and prints.

Stripe T-shirts

Plain T-shirts

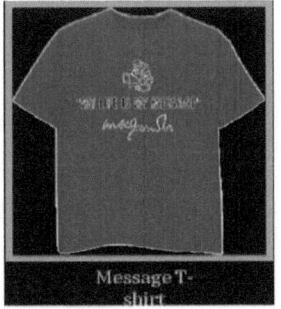
Message T-shirt

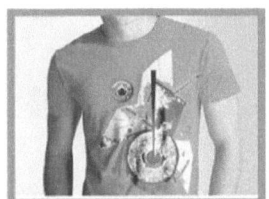
Graphic T-shirt

Men's casual Accessories

Casual Belt

Caps

Casual Shoes

Muffler

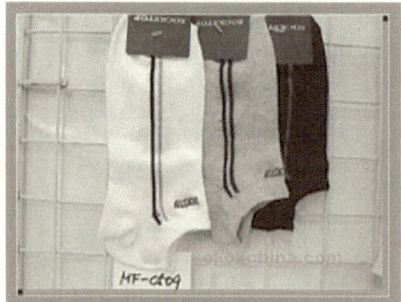

Socks

10.2 Women's Wear

Women have always been more aware about fashion than men and they spend a considerable time and money on clothing. Over the last century, women have seen major changes in their lifestyle. Women today lead multidimensional lives with many types of roles including that of a mother, wife, working women etc. Accordingly, their attire has a wide range of styles and fabric keeping their different roles in mind.

In India, even after the entry of British, sarees and salwar kameez remained the preferred dress for women. It's only in past 30 years or so, western formal tailored suits, skirt & gowns have made an entry in Indian women's wardrobe. With the beginning of the race of equality, the segmentation between the men's & women's wear has become blurred. Trouser suits have become preferred dress for office because it is much more comfortable. Jeans & shorts share the largest market share for casual attire. Saree are mostly used for function such as wedding etc or on festivals. They are also used as evening wear along with gowns. The Indian women apparel market has undergone a transformational phase over the past few years – growing number of working women, changing fashion trends, rising level of information and media exposure, and entry of large number of foreign brands have given the industry a new dimension. Below figure shows the division of women's wear category in various designs.

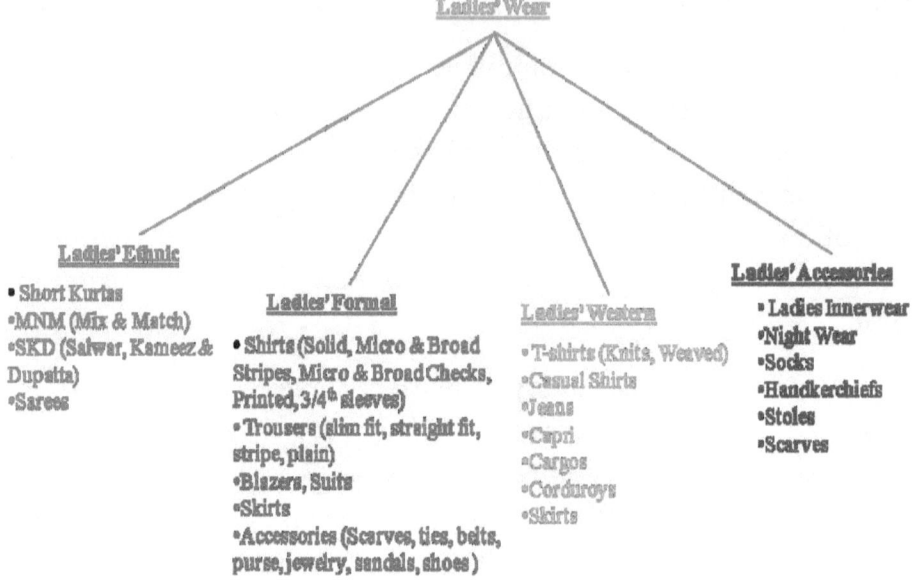

Ladies Ethnic

Short Kurta as shown beside looks nice on formal occasions but it defines various fashions statements too. Ladies kurta is a garment from India but getting popular in Western countries as well.

A woman may wear kurta with chudidars, with trousers or with jeans. Ladies kurtas are available in all shapes and sizes with several fashion patterns. Kurtis are in nowadays. They are available in different fabrics such as cotton, georgette and silk which allows it to be choice of all.

Salwar kameez is the traditional Indian clothing for women. Due to its high popularity in the region of Punjab, salwar kameez is commonly referred to as Punjabi suit. The fashion of Salwar Kameez in India is not new. Since the past many few centuries, women have been wearing this wonderful attire. Indian formal salwar kameez are unique in designs and have fine hand embroidery. Fabrics used for formal salwar kameez include chiffon, georgette, cotton and silk. Salwar Kameez looks great on all body types and sizes. Salwar Kameez come in many different styles such as Parallel/Trouser style salwar suits with a short Kurta style top, churidar style salwar kameez.

A Sari or Saree or Shari is a female garment in the Indian Subcontinent. The word 'sari' evolved from the Prakrit word 'sattika' as mentioned in earliest Jain and Buddhist literature. Saree is a marvel. It's a fine creation which gives that sensuous and caring touch, feminine appeal and above all aided by these factors gives its wearer, obviously a lady, that special sparkle and charm.

It fits with ease and comfort to the need of any woman since it is not cut nor tailored for any particular size. A chic modern woman looks elegant and neat in a Saree; hair cut short and trimmed projects the picture of a stylish Indian corporate office goer.

Ladies Formals

Ladies formal shirts are most suitable for office wear, business meetings and any other formal occasion. The choice of women formal shirts is endless and they offer a timeless look.

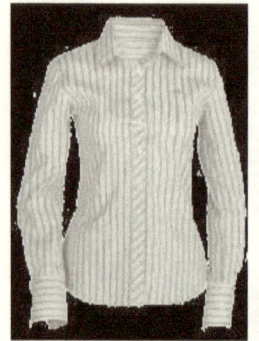

The best tailored formal shirts give a better fit and a modern look. Ladies formal shirts with its fabulous deep cuffs and beautiful buttons are the explanation of ultimate femininity.

These shirts usually have full sleeves, but they are also available with half sleeves, three-quarter length sleeves and even sleeveless. A wide range of fine quality and soft fabric is used for making formal shirts. The fabric is chosen in such a way that they are highly comfortable to wear and easy to fit.

Ladies formal trousers, as the name suggests, are meant for formal purposes like going to offices, formal and official parties, etc. These trousers demonstrate excellence and perfection when worn by any women of today.

Essential Characteristics:

- Length: These women trousers start from the waist and stops at the top or bottom of the foot.

- Waist Band: Waist bands are a hallmark of a women's formal trouser. They are the most common in formal trousers.

- Pleats: Women formal trousers may or may not have the pleats depending on the occasion.

- Pockets: The formal trousers for women may or may not have the pockets.

A variety of natural and synthetic fibers are used for the women formal trouser including Cotton, Wool and cotton blend, Polyester.

Apart from these, ladies formal category also includes formal blazers, suits and skirts as a part of daily formal wear.

There are many formal accessories used for ladies as below. These accessories add the value in look and style of the ladies formal.

Ladies Western

Various industry majors operating in men apparel segment have now started to diversify themselves into women wear in order to exploit the highly lucrative market.

Ladies western includes jeans, T-shirts, shirts, skirts, cargos, capris etc. Jeans were never out of fashion and will never ever be, all thanks to the very comfortable and durable denims. Available in a variety of dark and light shades, the jeans and tee trend is by far the most popular of the women's clothes trends. Long tops, short tops, t-shirts or tunics, all go extremely well with jeans. There is also the skinny jeans variety for juniors that have been very popular. Any kind of shoe or accessory will go well with them, as long as they are properly color coordinated.

There is no real end to the number of options available in trendy women's skirts. Be it the cut, the color or the length of the skirt, there are just too many to choose from. These include tie-dyed skirts, embellished gypsy skirts, foil skirts with beads, mini denim skirts, butterfly tiered skirts, etc. You can wear the different varieties of skirts with various tops and delicate jewelry and pumps.

T-shirt

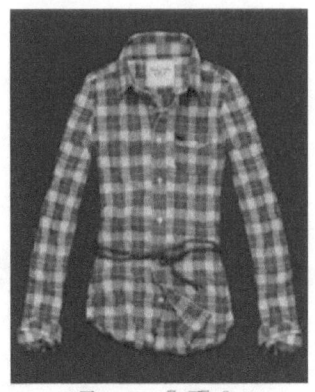
Casual Shirt

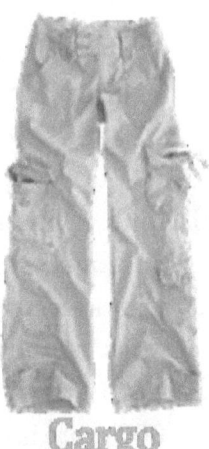
Cargo

Capri

10.3 Kid's Wear

Fashionable dresses for kids have witnessed a steady growth in the Indian market. Kids have become style conscious and love to dress up in unique and elegant dresses. Below is the division of kid's wear category.

Understanding Retail

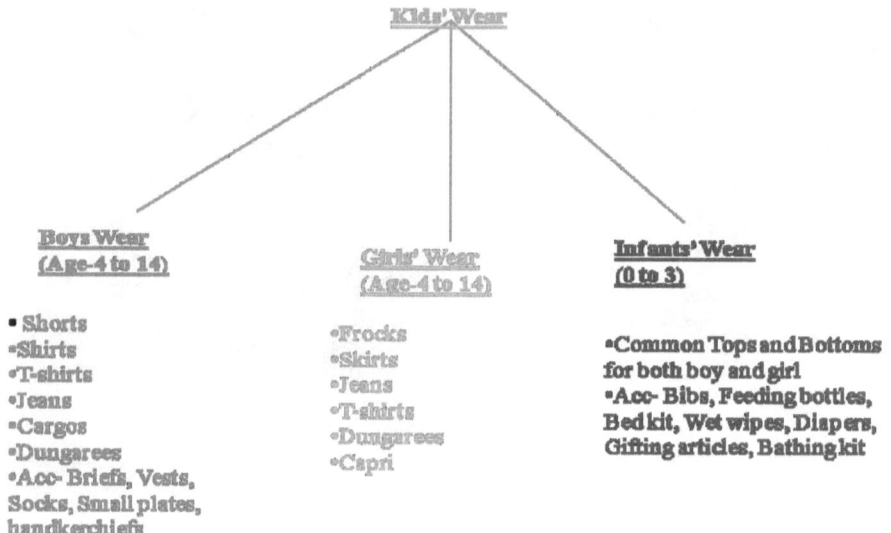

The kids' wear market is growing at the rate of 10% per annum, which makes it one of the fastest growing markets. There are two important factors to be considered for making a kids' apparel brand a success. They are variety and price. A children's apparel collection should have variety that will appeal to kids. Moreover, kids outgrow their clothes very rapidly. Hence it is necessary that kids' apparel range be reasonably priced. Children's apparel includes clothing for kids between 1 and 14 years of age. The market for kids' apparel in India exceeds Rs. 13,000 crore of which around Rs. 3,000 crore is constituted by branded kids' wear. According to Anil Lakhani, director of Gini & Jony, "the children's wear market constitutes 17% of the total Rs. 430 billion apparel industry, or about Rs. 73.1 billion, according to a study by KSA Technopak. Of this, the organized segment is only about 7% or over Rs. 5 billion.

Boys wear

Boys wear category has been mainly divided in to tops, bottoms and co-ordinates. Co-ordinates are also called as two pieces set.

Fashion Product Knowledge

Girls Wear

The market for girl's wear is greater than boy's wear. Boy's wear market concentrates on basic with a few designers capitalizing on fashion forward moms willing to spend money on their kids. Girls wear, however thrives in all channels from specialty stores to department stores to discounters.

Infant wear

The tiny footprints of infants are slowly but surely making an impact on the Indian clothing industry. With a growing amount of disposable income, in double income single child families, tailored or handmade clothes for infants are a thing of the past. The infant has become a valuable customer and clothing manufacturers are sitting up and taking notice of him.

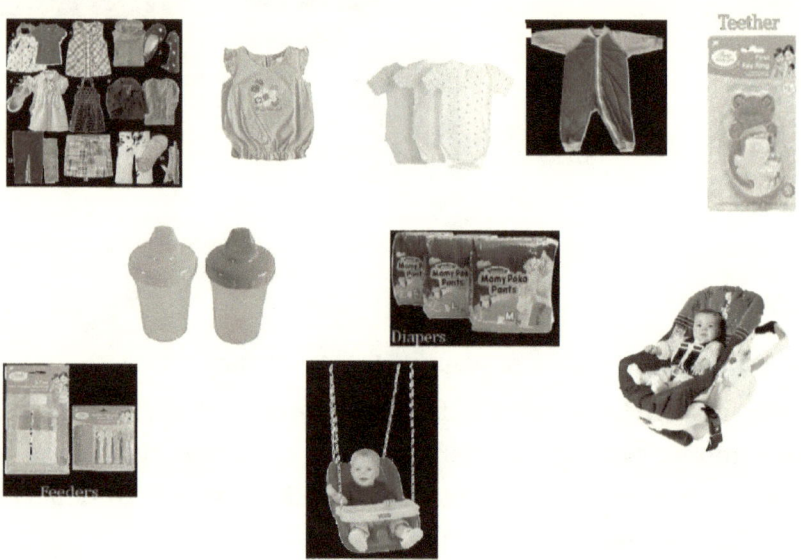

Kid's Ethnic wear

Ethnic wear in kids wear again follow the trends of men's wear & women's wear. Important factor which should be kept in mind while buying ethnic wear for kids should be comfort. Too much of embellishments etc might make the garment uncomfortable. The material used should also be such that it does not cause overheating. Kids' ethnic wear is comprised of –

- Salwar kameez
- Lehnga
- Sherwani & Dhoti kurta

11

Food and Non-Food Products and It Placement

 11.0 Objectives

After reading this unit, you should be able to know:

- The food category, its products and its placement
- The non-food category, its products and its placement

11.1 Introduction

Propelled by the increasing disposable income, the food sector has been witnessing a marked change in consumption pattern. Currently, India is the world's second largest producer of food in the world and the food processing industry is the one of the largest industries in India. In terms of production, consumption, export and expected growth, India is ranked fifth in the world. Below table shows the division of food and non food products.

Food	Non-Food
Fruits and Vegetables	Fast Moving Consumer Goods (FMCG)
Dairy	General Merchandise (Plastic, Utensils and Crockery)
Bakery	
Staples	
Fast Moving Consumer Goods (FMCG)	

11.2 Food Category

- **Fruits and Vegetables (F & V)**

"India's increasing population demands fruits and vegetables all year long. About 52% of India's workforce is directly involved in growing food and it is the second largest producer of fruits and vegetables in the world. The fruit and vegetable processing industry in India is highly decentralized having wide capacities. The diverse agro-climatic zones make it possible to grow almost all varieties of fresh fruits and green vegetables in India. India is the second largest producer of fresh vegetables in the world (ranks next to China) and accounts for about 15% of the world's production of vegetables.

According to national horticulture board the main fruits and vegetables grown in India are Apple, Banana, Lime/Lemon, Mosambi, Orange (Mandarin), Grapes, Mango, Papaya, Brinjal, Cabbage, Cauliflower, Okra, Onion, Peas, Potato and Tomato. In case of vegetables, potato, tomato, onion, cabbage and cauliflower account for around 60% of the total vegetable production in the country.

Although traditional fruits and vegetable vendors are the leaders in this market, modern sector is also growing very fast in this segment. Modern population of India prefers to buy vegetables and fruits from super markets for better pricing and less chances of cheating on prices. Below are some pictures to show the way Fruits and vegetables are being sold in super markets.

The above pictures show the way of displaying vegetables and fruits in a heaper style. In Heaper Display, products are neatly being arranged one above another.

This picture shows crates display. The baskets which are used to put vegetables are called crates. And the fixture on which these crates are displayed is called F & V Lounger.

This picture shows display of various vegetables in a chiller which will remain cool throughout the day. Generally this type of chiller display is done for international fruits and vegetables which can not remain good for long in normal Indian weather.

- **Dairy**

Dairy industry is of crucial importance to India. The country is the world's largest milk producer, accounting for more than 13% of world's total milk production. It is the world's largest consumer of dairy products, consuming almost 100% of its own milk production. Dairy products are a major source of cheap and nutritious food to millions of people in India and the only acceptable source of animal protein for large vegetarian segment of Indian population, particularly among the landless, small and marginal farmers and women. The huge volume of milk produced in India is consumed almost entirely by the Indian population itself, in a 50-50 division between urban and non-urban areas. Increasingly, important consumers of the dairy industry are fast-food chains and food and non-food industries using dairy ingredients in a wide range of products.

Below are pictures of dairy chiller and freezer. It stores all the dairy products in a cold condition. These items are segregated according to its product class and arranged neatly in the shown chiller or freezer.

- **Bakery**

Bakery industry in India is the largest of the food industries with an annual turnover of about Rs. 3000 crores. India is the second largest producer of biscuits after USA. The biscuit industry in India comprises of traditional and modern sectors. Bread and Biscuits form the major baked foods accounting for over 80% of total bakery products produced in the country. The quantities of bread and biscuits produced are more or less the same. However, value of biscuits is more than bread. The industry has traditionally been and largely continues to be in the unorganized sector contributing over 70% of the total production. Bakery products once considered as sick man's diet, have now become an essential food items of the vast majority of population.

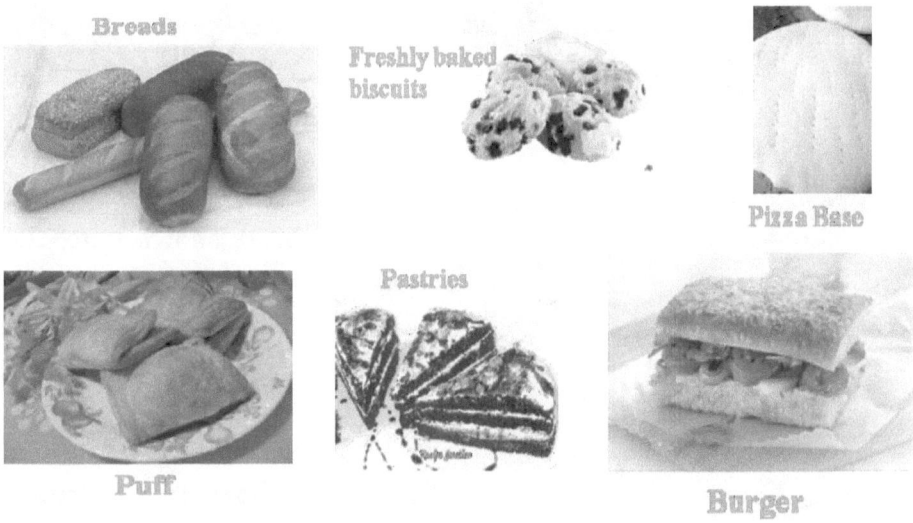

- **Staples**

Staples is one of the biggest food category. It consist of different cereals, pulses, spices, wheat floor, rice etc.

Cereals

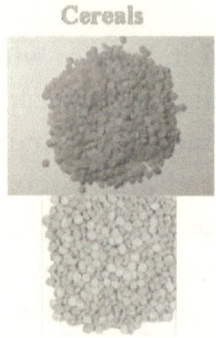

Rice

Wheat floor

Pulses

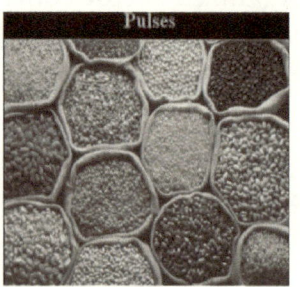

Spices

This picture shows the display of loose staples. As shown here, the staples are being stocked in drums in the store. Sometimes heapers display is also done in case of packaged staples. Heaper display will be done according to the size of packets as shown in the picture.

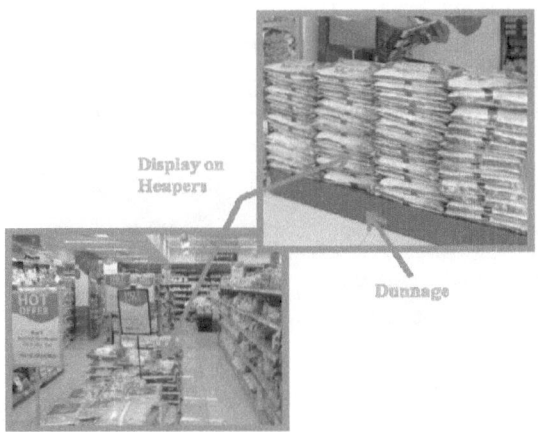

Staple's display on shelves

- **FMCG (Fast Moving Consumer Goods) Food**

FMCG are products that are sold quickly and at relatively low cost. Examples include non-durable goods such as soft drinks and grocery items. Though the absolute profit made on FMCG products is relatively small, they generally sell in large quantities, so the cumulative profit on such products can be large.

Display on Gondola

Display on bays on wall

Above picture shows the fixtures and placement of FMCG Food products.

11.3 Non-Food Category

Non-food category includes both FMCG products and general merchandise.

- **FMCG Non-Food**

FMCG non-food products are fast moving daily used products like soaps, shampoos, detergents, creams, toiletries etc. Some of the FMCG Non-food products are shown below.

Display of FMCG Non-food product is done on the shelves of wall and gondolas.

- **General Merchandise**

General Merchandise category refers to the products like home appliances, utensils, crockery, plastic products etc. some of the example of general merchandise are as below.

12

Known and Unknown Loss Management

 12.0 Objectives

After reading this unit, you should be able to know:

- What is known loss and its causes?
- What is unknown loss and its causes?

12.1 Introduction

In the retail environment, there are many causes of loss. Some type of loss will be treated as known loss where a loss occurs that can clearly have its reason captured – eg: where product goes out of date and is removed from store. Other types of loss will be treated as unknown loss where it is not possible for a retailer to attribute a definitive reason to the loss. eg: expected stock is found to be missing during stock take. Some retailers may treat the various loss types differently to others. This will depend on their internal processes and capabilities to differentiate loss types, and potentially their corporate administration requirements.

12.2 Known Loss

Known loss is the loss of stock identified as being unfit to sell to customers. This loss is known to the store. It cannot always be a financial loss to the store. Below are some examples of known loss.

112 Understanding Retail

SPOILT – refrigeration malfunction

BROKEN – glass has been smashed

SPILT – liquids can leak from packaging

DAMAGED – accidentally dropped product

DATE EXPIRED PRODUCT – product out of shelf life

- **Causes of known loss**

Most loss is driven by a particular event that changes the quality of a product as below.

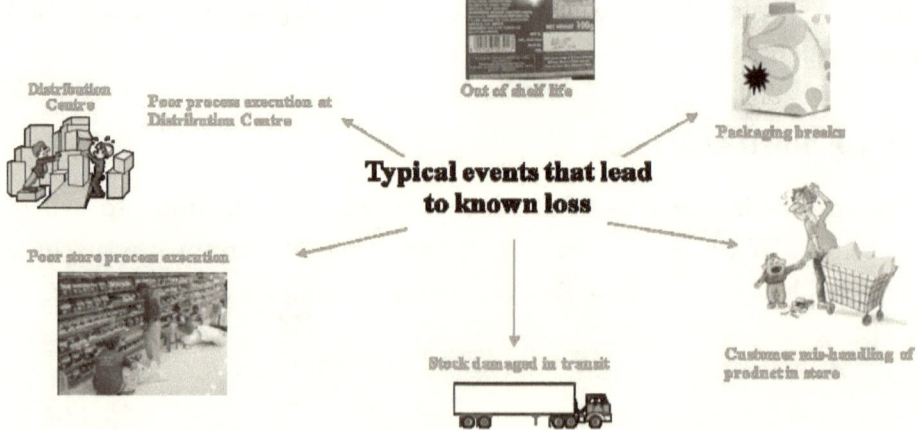
Typical events that lead to known loss:
- Poor process execution at Distribution Centre
- Out of shelf life
- Packaging breaks
- Poor store process execution
- Stock damaged in transit
- Customer mis-handling of product in store

Due to poor handling of the product at various stages of supply chain like warehouse, distribution centre, at the store back room and while displaying on shelves, the product may get damaged. Packaging breaks, mishandling by the customers, expiry date are some other examples of known loss happening at the stores. Known loss can take place anywhere in the store and the challenge is to identify them all to reduces loses.

12.3 Unknown Loss

Unknown loss is also known as Shrinkage/Pilferage in the industry. It has a direct impact to a store's Profit & Loss. It is critical to manage and minimise unknown loss for store's financial health. Shrink is the reduction of stock value due to unknown causes. It is measured in Rupees and is a derived figure in the accounting books. Shrink management is about taking steps to prevent the figure from increasing.

How does shrink occur?

- Customer theft – Physical
- Staff theft – People
- Vendor theft – DSD
- Short deliveries – Inventory
- Stock counting errors
- Paperwork errors

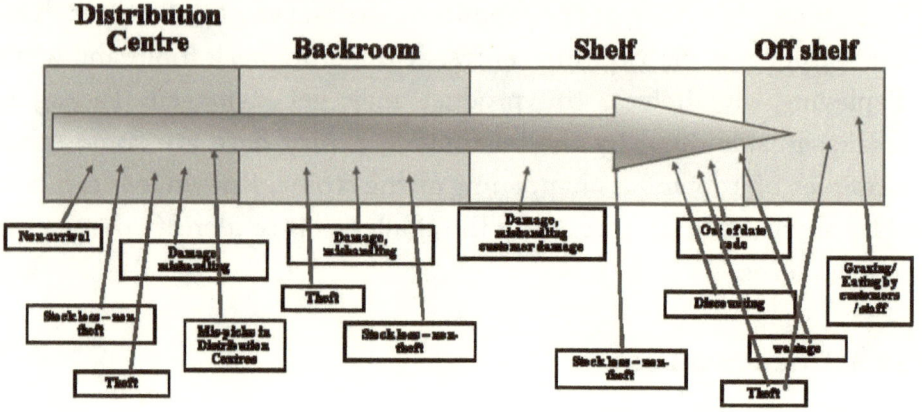

The failure to control and minimise losses means a direct loss to the store

1. Loss of profit
2. Loss of trade
3. Stock replacement
4. Negative wastage

As shown above, unknown loss results in to a financial loss and affects the bottom line of the business. The store management has to identify the causes of unknown loss, develop a system to control it and reduce such loses.

13

Staff and Customer Safety

 13.0 Objectives

After reading this unit, you should be able to know:

- The methods of maintaining Food hygiene
- Emergency Response Techniques (ERT) and safe working practices

13.1 Introduction

Customer safety is important for all businesses. Customers must have a safe experience while making a purchase or while waiting for a service to be completed. An adequate amount of signs around the store or work zone will show the potential risks while shopping or waiting for a service. The signs should be placed in areas that are easily seen by people, such as next to doorways. For example, retail stores that have sliding glass entry and exit doors should have signs mentioning to customers that the doors are automatic and may close on them if the sensor doesn't detect movement. Customers should be the first ones out of the store or service area during an emergency, such as a fire. During an emergency, all employees should notify and assist customers out of the store in a safe, timely fashion. The store or service area should be checked throughout to ensure that no customers were left behind. Signs around doorways should identify emergency exits. By maintaining cleanliness standards of the store, many contaminations can also be avoided.

13.2 Food Hygiene

Maintaining food hygiene in the store is to give assurance to the customers that food will not cause any harm to them when it is prepared and/or eaten according to its intended use.

As a food handler, a person is responsible for protecting and ensuring the safety of food. His role is to:

1. Maintain cleanliness
2. Protect food from contamination
3. Follow good hygiene habits

There are many causes of contamination as shown below.

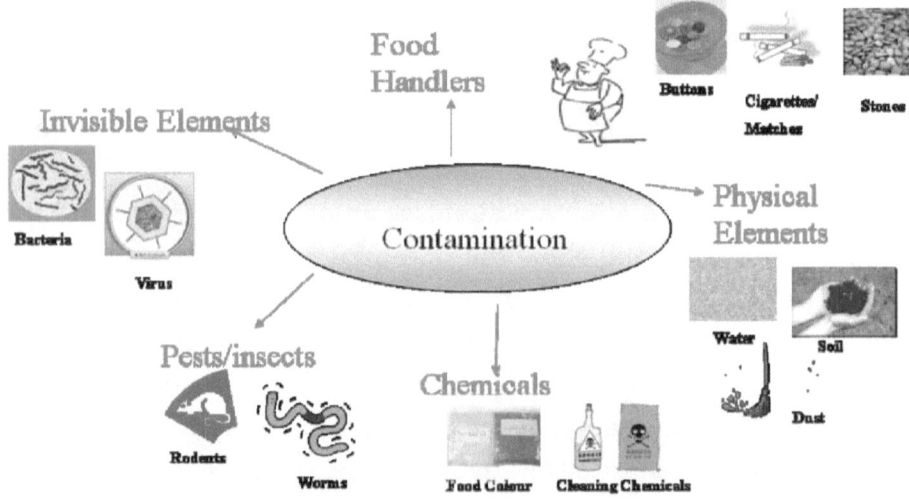

- **Follow "Clean as you go" principle**

Maintain cleanliness of the

- Shop floor – Floor, Fixtures, Trolleys & Baskets
- Backroom – Dustbins, backroom furniture and other peripherals

- Electrical Equipment – Lights, Exhaust Fans, Air Curtains, Chillers, Freezers
- Forecourt Area – Lights, Signages, Dustbins

To prevent contamination,

a. Wear protective clothing like Head gear, Food handling gloves, Apron etc.

b. Avoid opening packaging near food products

c. Do not keep pens or other items in pocket

d. Wash hands every time

e. Keep all food contact surfaces & equipment clean, sanitised and in good condition

f. Use only company approved cleaning products and follow manufacturer instructions

g. Do not store non-food products with food products

- **Food safety while delivery**

When inspecting incoming food checks for:

a. Unusual appearance or smell/variation in colour, texture, odour or general appearance

b. Signs of frozen food thawing

c. Signs of pest infestation or activity

d. Damage to packaging

- **Food safety while storage**

a. Keep highly perishable food under refrigeration

b. Keep other products under cool, dry and well ventilated conditions

   c. Make sure there is sufficient space between products

   d. Ensure secure packaging

   e. Keep stocks on dunnage (palate) of at least 6 inches above the ground

   f. Rotate stock

- **Waste Disposal**

Correct rubbish disposal:

   a. Bins should be emptied outside of processing areas and at frequent intervals

   b. After emptying, containers should be cleaned

   c. Use bin liners

   d. Wash hands after emptying

During rubbish disposal, Never:

   a. Wear protective clothing

   b. Wear food handling gloves

- **Food Disposal**

   a. Always dispose out of date stock

   b. Always dispose or return damaged or defective food produce

   c. Always keep food for disposal segregated from sellable food

   d. Food waste must always be recorded in shrink logs to manage replenishment of stock

13.3 Emergency Response Techniques (ERT) and Safe Working Practices

- **Electrical Safety**

Loose cables can cause

   a. Tripping hazards

   b. Electrocution

   c. Damage to equipment

Do not use frayed extension cords!

- **Floor Safety**

Working Environment

   a. Keep aisles clear of obstacles that can cause staff, customers or visitors to trip and fall e.g. trolleys, stock, rubbish, packaging, and boxes

   b. Store exits, fire exits and stairs must be accessible at all times

   c. Check for sharp, dangerous edges on fixtures

   d. Ensure steps are not slippery

   e. Spills and dropped food must be cleaned immediately

   f. Use the 'Wet Floor' sign

   g. All floors and floor coverings must be maintained to company standards to ensure people can't trip or slip

   h. Take care when entering/exiting doorways – do not rush, watch for other people, especially if carrying goods

Counter tops

   a. Point of sale areas should be clean and tidy to prevent accidents

b. Area around cash drawer should be free to ensure staff are not knocked when drawer extends

c. All electrical connections and loose wires should be bound together to prevent entangling or electrical accidents

d. Machineries and equipment should not be used prior to training and guidance in its use

Hazardous Substances

a. All hazardous cleaning substances should be stored away from customer access

b. In case spillage of any hazardous substance occurs, special precautions need to be taken

- **Accident Reporting**

Report all accidents to Store Manager, Supervisor or Human Resources Watch out for unsafe conditions, and report them to Supervisor

- **First Aid**

Make sure that you know the location of the nearest First Aid Kit Make sure that the First Aid Kit is stocked properly Ensure no expired medicine is kept in the First Aid Kit

- **Responsibilities in Fire Situations**

a. Recognize a fire condition

b. Activate the fire alarm system

c. Evacuate the building

d. Call 101 to report the fire condition and to make sure help is on the way

e. Remember you are not a trained fire fighter. You should never put your life in danger

f. Ensure to stick to your presence of mind in emergency situations

g. Keep your head calm

h. Know the exits!

i. Do not run to exits, but walk to exits!

j. Ensure easy access to the safest way out!

14

Selling Skills

 ## 14.0 Objective

After reading this unit, you should be able to know:

- The background and history of selling
- The various Methods and Techniques in Retail Selling
- How to identify needs of customer
- Selling of High end products
- Closing of sale

14.1 Introduction

While it was once considered there are only born salesman, training and development process has produced several millions of salesman worldwide. Alfred Tack in UK opened several schools called "Alfred Tack School for Selling" and has over 6 decades of history to it. It is always also argued as to whether selling is a "Art or Science". Experts say that while selling is an ART, the success of selling is in understanding the science or essence of every product to be sold and convince customer. Therefore selling is both art and science.

14.2 History of Selling the Tack Way

Two brothers, George and Alfred Tack, established the original TACK Company in London in 1948. The company formed part of a diversified group known as the TACK Organisation. TACK Training was born out of the brothers' first venture, a business called NuAire. The company specialized in heating and ventilation systems and, with George an engineer and Alfred a salesman, the brothers were well placed to make the venture a success.

Alfred, a charismatic entrepreneur, soon realized that to stay ahead of the competition they needed to train their sales team in the art of professional selling, a groundbreaking approach! Before long news of this new phenomenon, known as Sales Training, spread and other companies asked if they could come along and benefit from the training themselves. George and Alfred charged them a guinea to attend and TACK Training was born!

1955 – The start of TACK's international network

TACK continues to lead the training market both in the UK and internationally. It is the only training organisation with such an extensive international network of partners, providing its customers with the same consistently high quality of training and development worldwide. The first overseas partner was recruited in 1955 and since then the TACK Worldwide network has increased to 50 countries with training provided in 25 languages. Alfred tack books on selling are most popular and bible for every salesman.

14.3 Methods in Selling:

There are several method and techniques of selling; however the research has finally found the following techniques to be most popular and acceptable in Retail selling.

1. **BSA Method** – **B**ackground Information, **S**pecific Area of Concern, **A**greement to need

2. **Spin Selling** – Neil Rackham method of "Hurt & Rescue"

3. **FAB Technique** – **F**eature, **A**dvantage, **B**enefits

4. **TFE Technique** – **T**ouch, **F**eel and **E**xperience

BSA Method:

This technique was perfected by a leading U.S. University and is taught to a number of Sales Personnel worldwide. The BSA method is a scientifically proven method of selling to a customer walking in. It does not pressurize the customer but gently leads him into the sale.

In this technique a sales person selling a consumer durable, Electronics or even a luxury label in Apparel will give the customer the background information about the company, their other popular range of products, warranty/Guarantee for the product. The customer will be influenced and willing to consider the product.

However he will express his "Area of Concern" like after sales service if it is a consumer durable or electronic, or about colour fastness in apparel, also will express about the implication of Guarantees or Warranty. The sales person has to clear this area of concern in most convincing way which will lead to "Agreement of Need". That is customer will feel that the said product is meeting his/her Need and criteria's.

SPIN Selling

Neil Rackham, in his classic book shows how classic sales techniques such as closing and objection-handling can actually reduce your chance of selling, especially in big business-to-business sales situations, where buyers are savvy to the classic tricks.

Overall, the method, like many other approaches, is a 'hurt and rescue' approach. You find their problem and 'hurt' them by exposing the terrible things that might happen (spot the use of tension). Then you rescue them with your product. The four question types are described below.

Situation questions

In big sales, minimize the small talk and focus on finding background detail that can be used to make sense of the buyer's business situation. Context creates meaning. This is about understanding the wider context before you zoom into the details.

Problem questions

Ask questions to uncover problems which your product can address. If you are selling tractors, ask about maintenance costs, breakdowns and so on. If you are selling life insurance, ask about how many dependents the person has.

A trap here is to dive straight into presenting the benefits of what you are selling. You may know the problem, but they do not! Going straight to the sales pitch will just get you objections.

Implication questions

Instead of telling them the problem they have (which is also likely to raise objections), the goal is now to get them to see (and feel!) the problem. By asking questions which draw out the implications of the problem, they get to feel the pain that will drive them towards your product. This is the 'hurt' of Hurt and Rescue.

For example, the person selling tractors might ask about implications of unploughed fields whilst the life insurance salesperson could carefully ask what would happen to the children if the target person died or became very ill.

Need-Payoff questions

Having hurt the target person with your implications, you now give them a straw to grasp at by asking how their pain could be resolved. With careful questions, you can get them to the state where they are asking for your product even before you show it to them. This is a very neat 'rescue' of Hurt and Rescue, where they either rescue themselves or ask you to rescue them.

For example, the tractor sales person can ask how much better the tractor was like when it was new, or whether any of the farmer's neighbours have solved problems of old and problematic tractors. The insurance sales person could ask questions that build pictures of the target person's children being safe and secure whatever curve-balls the world might throw at the family.

FAB Technique in Selling

Feature, Advantage and Benefit of a product for example a washing machine have to explained to customer clearly for him/her to take a decision. Let's assume the customer wants to buy a fully automatic washing machine.

Feature: Fully automatic washing machine are available in two systems of wash, one is front loading machine like IFB, Samsung, LG etc and another Top loading model. Within front loading and top loading there are different sizes and capacity of load that can be washed. Washing machine have different dimension in size and shape and it is necessary to check the space and facility available for fully automatic washing machine.

Advantage: While explaining the advantages the salesman needs to understand the need of the customer on the number of people in the family. What is the likely duration of washing of the clothes, like daily, alternate day, once in three days etc? Based on these criteria he/she should recommend the right brand of machines with its distinct advantages.

Benefit: The benefits will be mostly the guarantee on the product, number of years of guarantee or warranty, Colour options available, add-on such as free fittings or free installation and delivery of the product to customer. Schemes like lucky draw scratch card or free annual maintenance.

TFE Technique in Selling:

Most modern retailing allows the customer to **Touch, Feel and Experience of merchandise.** In lifestyle stores like Shoppers Stop, Lifestyle, Westside, Pantaloon, Total etc customer can touch the product, fabric and feel the texture, finish and appreciate the product. Customer also can take apparel into the trial room and wear to experience the finish, fit and look of the product and decide to buy.

In electronics and consumer durables customer can get demo of the product and see the performance and in products like mobile phones and music systems/Television etc they can get comparative features and advantages and price comparisons instantly and then take the decision to buy.

In automobile sector the touch feel and experience comes in the form of test drives for the customer and only condition being that he/she should produce a valid driving license.

Touch, Feel and Experience is modern retailing's respect to CUSTOMER acknowledging their importance to commerce.

Customer Centered Selling

This is the approach used by Xerox, where author Robert Jolles sold and taught for a number of years, and is one of the few books that take selling beyond the stage of 'Here's what I learned in 30 years of selling.' It uses an eight stage process, as below. The dual titles indicate what the customer/sales person is doing at each stage.

1. Satisfaction/research

Customers at this stage are happy with the products they have. The sales person uses this period to research the customer:

- Seeking problems which may be addressed by the product.
- Finding people who will influence the purchase decision.
- Building relationships that will help the sale later on.

Questions are deliberately used to determine the context (like SPIN 'Situation' questions) and plant the seeds for later stages.

Identified problems are not highlighted at this stage, as this will only elicit objections.

2. Acknowledgement/analysis

At this stage, customers acknowledge that they have a problem, but may well not see it as being worth solving. They will happily spend a very long time in this stage.

The sales person seeks to get the person to the next stage by getting them to see the problem as worth solving, by:

- Asking Identification Probes questions to identify the problem.
- Asking Development Probes to identify the full extent of the current problem.
- Asking Impact Probes to get them to feel the pain of future problem.

Note the close parallels with the SPIN 'Problem' and 'Implication' questions.

3. Decision/confirmation

Now the customer has decided to solve their problem, but is still nowhere near selecting your product.

The sales person quickly verifies that the customer wants to solve the problem, checks for any other concerns and ensures they are ready to move on.

4. Criteria/requirement

The customer now decides on the criteria to use to select the final solution.

The sales person guides this process by eliciting the appropriate and prioritizing the needs that are behind the identified problem and which will lead towards the right decision.

5. Measurement/specification

The customer here turns the criteria into a coherent measure of what will constitute success. In particular, they are asking, 'What will it take to fix the problem?'

The sales person guides the transferring of the identified needs/criteria into a clear specification, and ensures the customer is committed to it.

6. Investigation/solution

The customer now goes looking for a product to meet the specification they (and hopefully the sales person).

The sales person checks that if they can meet the specification then the customer will give them the sale ('If I...would you...' trial close). After dealing with any objections, the target solution is presented, using the FABEC sequence:

- Show Features that meet customer needs (in priority order).
- Show additional Advantages.

- Describe Benefits that the customer is really buying.
- Explain how it works (but don't overdo it!).
- Confirm that they are comfortable with all of this.

7. Selection/close

The customer now makes the final selection of the product to meet their specification and criteria and hence solve their problems.

The sales person summarizes benefits (Summary Close), asks for the sale (using their favorite close), discusses any logistics detail and reassures the customer that they have made a good decision.

8. Reconsideration/maintenance

The customer now takes delivery, uses the product and eventually comes around to buying a replacement.

The sales person should keep an eye on the whole delivery, setup and training to ensure that the customer stays satisfied in those crucial early days. It also helps to check that the solution really did solve the customer's problem. And staying in touch on an ongoing basis enables you to spot any future opportunities.

Relationship selling

The problem with one-off selling in a situation where you want the customer to come back again is that if they are at all unhappy then will go elsewhere next time. Worse still, they may warn their friends not to buy from you either. The preferred alternative for many sales situations is to build the right relationship.

Relationship selling is also known by other names, including 'Consultative Selling'.

It's the people!

An important part of selling where you want repeat sales is the relationship between the sales person and the person doing the buying. If the person is going to buy often, then the relationship may even develop into a genuine friendship.

The centrality of trust

In a relationship-based situation, a critical factor is trust. This takes time to build, for particularly for the buyer to accept that the seller will always keep their best interests at heart. If trust is threatened or broken, then the sales person will have to put in a huge effort to rescue the relationship – and even then it may be lost.

Whereas in One-off selling the buyer has most to lose, in relationship selling the seller can be the biggest loser if they sell something that is not wanted. Not only may the product be returned, but all future sales may be lost.

Trust-building is such a major activity in this approach it can take up to half of your time. But this is repaid by a short close (as opposed the long objection-handling of one-off selling).

Win-win

This type of selling has to end up as a variable-pie win-win exchange. The seller wants the buyer to feel that they have got a fair deal, and the buyer, although they want a good price, do not want the seller to go out of business. Many negotiable beyond price are on the table, including goodwill and future sales opportunities.

Relationship selling happens in any place where relationships are important. Thus when a husband and wife are negotiating about something, they will be more successful if they both consider the relationship as well as whatever it is they each want.

Sales tips:

What makes a sales person successful? Success in sales depends upon some basics. A few pointers for success in sales:

1. Be sincere with people. Too many sales people act in a manner that seems artificial or they only feign interest in their prospects' problems and concerns. People are smart and see right through such insincerity. If you are not sincere and honest with everyone you meet then you should not be in sales.

2. It is vitally important to constantly hone your sales and communications skills. Continuous growth and training in formal professional selling techniques is also very important. Take training classes, listen to audio cassette professional development tapes, read all the professional development material you can get your hands on, and start a program of self-study and development in sales today if you haven't already.

3. First listen to your customer, understand his or her wants and needs, and only then try to determine whether or not you can deliver the product or services to meet those wants and needs. If you approach a prospect with a solution before understanding the problem you are likely to be wrong about the solution.

4. The best sales people ask a lot of questions and genuinely listen to the answers before speaking again.

5. Your prospects and customers are all different so you should treat them differently.

6. The best sales people listen much more than they talk.

7. Find out what your prospects want and then give it to them.

8. If you cannot give your prospects what they want, tell them so and help them find what they are looking for elsewhere.

9. If you think that you cannot make it in sales as a profession, then you probably should not even try.

It should be noted that while we present these activities in an order that is suggestive of a step-by-step approach (i.e., one activity must be carried out before the next); in many selling situations this will not be the case. For example, a buyer for a large retailer may have observed a salesperson's product being used while visiting a competitor's store. The buyer, anxious to obtain the product for use in her own stores, contacts the salesperson immediately upon returning to the office. After addressing a few questions from the salesperson confirming the buyer's status at the retail company and without much prodding by the salesperson, the buyer places an order and agrees to meet the salesperson for lunch the next day. In our example, only activities #2 – Qualifying the Lead, #6 – Closing the Sale and #7 – Account Maintenance are carried out in order to obtain the sale and to begin building a long-term relationship.

Additionally, salespeople often find circumstances in which all activities are required but the order these are carried out may be disrupted. For instance, salespeople are often confronted with a buyer who is resistant to making a purchase even before the salesperson has made a presentation (e.g., "I don't think I'm interested in what you're selling"). This will likely force the salesperson to adjust his or her selling process. In this example it will require the salesperson address the buyer's resistance before beginning to present the product, which may occur in activities associated with either Preparation for the Sales Call or The Sales Meeting.

Preparation for the Sales Call

If a prospect has been qualified or if qualifying cannot take place until additional information is obtained (e.g., when first talking to the prospect), a salesperson's next task is to prepare for an eventual sales call. This activity in the selling process has two main objectives:

Learn More about the Customer

While during the lead generation and qualifying portion of the selling process a seller may have gained a great deal of knowledge about a customer, invariably there is much more to be known that will be helpful once an actual sales call is made. The salesperson will use their research skills to learn about such issues as:

- who is the key decision maker
- what is the customer's organizational structure
- what products are currently being purchased
- how are purchase decisions made

Salespeople can attempt to gather this information through several sources including: corporate research reports, information on the prospect's website, conversations with non-competitive salespeople who have dealt with the prospect, website forums where industry information is discussed, and by asking questions when setting up sales meetings (see Arranging Prospect Contact). Gaining this information can help prepare the salesperson for the sales presentation. For example, if the salesperson learns which competitor currently supplies the prospect then the salesperson can tailor promotional material in a way that compares the seller's products against products being purchased by the prospect. Additionally, having more information about a prospect allows the salesperson to be more confident in his/her presentation and, consequently, come across as more knowledgeable when meeting with the prospect.

14.4 Closing the Sale

Most people involved in selling acknowledge that this part of the selling process is the most difficult. Closing the sale is the point when the seller asks the prospect to agree to make the purchase. It is also the point at which many customers are unwilling to make a commitment and, consequently, respond to the seller's request by saying no. For anyone involved in sales such rejection can be very difficult to overcome, especially if it occurs on a consistent basis.

Yet the most successful salespeople will say that closing the sale is actually fairly easy if the salesperson has worked hard in developing a relationship with the customer. Unfortunately some buyers, no matter how satisfied they are with the seller and their product, may be insecure or lack confidence in making buying decisions. For these buyers, salespeople must rely on persuasive communication skills that help assist and even persuade a buyer to place an order.

The use of persuasive communication techniques is by far the most controversial and most misunderstood concept related to the selling process. Why? Because to many people the act of persuasion is viewed as an attempt to manipulate someone into doing something they really do not want to do. However, for sales professionals this is not what persuasive communication is about. Instead, persuasion is a skill for assisting someone in making a decision; it is not a technique for making someone make a decision. The difference is important. Where one is manipulative, the other is helpful and designed to benefit the buyer. And as we noted, persuasion does not always occur. Many times buyers take the lead in closing a sale since they are convinced the product is right for them.

For salespeople, understanding when it is time to close a sale and what techniques should be used takes experience. In any event, the close is not the end of the selling process but is the beginning of building a relationship.

15

Customer Relationship Management

 15.0 Objective

After reading this unit, you should be able to know:

- History of CRM
- Customer Behaviour & CRM
- What is Loyalty Card?
- What is Consumer Profiling?
- Be aware of follow up after the closing the sale
- Ask questions and clarify objection
- Breaking the "Alliance" in a sale

15.1 Introduction

Customer relationship management is a broadly recognized, widely implemented strategy for managing and nurturing a company's interactions with clients and sales prospects. It involves using technology to organize, automate, and synchronize business processes— principally sales activities, but also those for marketing, customer service, and technical support. The overall goals are to find, attract, and win new clients, nurture and retain those the company already has, entice former clients back into the fold, and reduce the costs of marketing and client service. Once simply a label for a category of software tools, today, it generally denotes a company-wide business strategy embracing all client-facing departments and even beyond. When an implementation is effective, people, processes, and technology work in synergy to increase profitability, and reduce operational costs. Customer relationship management is the system that is responsible for introducing things such as frequent flyer gifts and credit card points. Before CRM, this was rarely done. Customers would simply buy from the company, and little was done to maintain their relationship. Before the introduction of CRM, many companies, especially those that were in the Fortune 500 category, didn't feel the need to cater to the company.

15.2 History of CRM

Customer Relationship Management originated years before the start of the first millennium in Mesopotamia. Farmers who were eager to sell their surplus produce became the first initiators of the customer oriented processes are now familiar with.

With the passage of time and the first millennium an accurate record of transactions was kept by the merchants accounting for what was sold and whom it was sold to. This list of customers provided the first comprehensive customer oriented data and proved to be the beginning of customer oriented strategies. The advent of the 1990's however saw a more refined customer oriented implementation taking place, laying the ground for the CRM strategy as we now know it.

Tesco was instrumental in bringing this about. Dunnhumms collaboration with it due to the influence of Edwina Dunn and Clive proved to be the foundation for CRM. Since these two individuals had realized the importance of knowing and understanding their customers, they understood the supreme need for adopting the right customer approach.

Tesco, the second largest grocer in the UK implemented a customer loyalty program used in 12 of their stores. Known as the Tesco Club Card Program it focused entirely on the customer and implemented the necessary business activity changes with the customer in view. While doing this it assisted in the collation of the information about customer preferences and the net result was amazing. Profits soared, competitors complained and Tesco reigned supreme. Its additional focus on customers proved to be the focal point of success. Watching competitors realized that this was but the right approach to adopt and that it generated huge funds. They realized that customer retention and customer loyalty were but a natural by-product. Realization that this approach was the right one and its subsequent implementation by Tesco was CRM's launch in the world wide market. From then on it was smooth sailing for CRM. Hailed as the customer strategy of the decade CRM was the new option for organizations. Initially CRM focused less on big industries and far more on small and medium industries. Since the revenue from large corporate was higher it was felt that these industries should be the focal point. With the passing of time this notion changed and the importance of focusing on medium and small industries was noted. Today CRM solutions have turned CRM into a necessary commodity for medium to small businesses and are being implemented in a wide range of industries. Various vendor solutions have been improvised catering to a vast area.

15.3 Consumer Behaviour & CRM

'What' products and services do we buy, 'why' do we buy, 'how often' do we buy, from 'where do we buy, 'how do we buy, etc. are the issues which are dealt with in the discipline of consumer behaviour. Consumer behaviour can be defined as those acts of individuals (consumers) directly involved in obtaining, using, and disposing of economic goods and services, including the decision processes that precede and determine these acts. Just by human nature, consumers can be spontaneous, unpredictable, and selfish.

One thing that we have in common is that we are all consumers. In fact everybody in this world is a consumer. Everyday of our life we are buying and consuming an incredible variety of goods and services. However, we all have different tastes, likes and dislikes and adopt different behaviour patterns while making purchase decisions. One may preferred to use Colgate toothpaste, Dove soap, Head & Shoulder shampoo while your spouse may prefer another type for same requirement. Similarly, you may have a certain set of preferences in food, clothing, books, magazines, recreational activities, forms of savings and the stores from where you prefer to shop, which may be different not only from those of your spouse but also your friends, neighbours and colleagues. Each consumer is unique and this uniqueness is reflected in the consumption behaviour and pattern and process of purchase. The study of consumer behaviour provides us with reasons why consumers differ from one another in buying and using products and services. Customers and their behaviours comprise of many attributes and differentials. These differences are not just associated with demographics, groups or any one particular item. There is a complex development of behaviours that exist in the consumer markets.

In the world we live today, businesses and top Marketing executives must understand what differentiates their companies or their products from others and must understand the needs of the consumers in their markets. If they able to understand their product and consumer's need, than it's very easy for them to develop a strategic plan and create a market niche and develop their customer base with very good customer relations. Customer Relationship Management can help them to take competitive advantage in the market. Customer Relations depend on understanding the customer and their reactions to the environment which will at last prolong the life of customer relationship between company and their customers. Understanding the customer need can be a starting point for majority businesses. There are possibilities of gap occurs between customers expectation and what businesses think customers expect. It results into overlook or not understanding customer's perceptions and real requirement. Profiling the market should be a top priority while setting up a retail shop. Even for existing store it is important to continuously monitor the market if the store has to stay in touch with the customer. It might also be useful to look at any changes in marketplace before contemplating changing the direction or focus of a store. This will help to gauge the chance of success or simply show if there are any emerging markets in the geographical area.

15.4 Role of Loyalty Card as a CRM Tool

In marketing generally and in retailing more specifically, a loyalty card, rewards card, point's card, or club card is a plastic or paper card, visually similar to a credit card or debit card that identifies the card holder as a member in a commercial incentives programme. Loyalty cards are a system of the loyalty business model. In the United Kingdom and India it is typically called a loyalty card, in Australia a rewards card or a points card, and in the United States either a discount card, a club card or a rewards card. Cards typically have a barcode or magstripe or an EPROM chip that can be easily scanned, and some are even chip cards. Small key ring cards are often used for convenience. There are generally six types of loyalty programmes:

- **Appreciation:** Giving customers more of a company's product/service
- **Rewards:** Rewarding customers unrelated to a company's product/service
- **Partnerships:** Marketing to another company's database and allowing loyal customers to choose their rewards from either company.
- **Rebate**: Giving discount on the purchased product to the customers.

- **Affinity**: Building a lifetime value relationship with a customer based on mutual interests and not on the use of rewards

- **Coalition:** Teaming up with different companies to share customer data to jointly target a specific customer demographic.

- A customer loyalty card is instrumental in bringing some advantages. It works for:

- **Repeat purchases:** When an apparel brand announces special discounts on its products or services, customers using the brand's loyalty cards are informed about the benefits of the scheme. This in turn maximizes the chance of repeat purchases as a customer who gets special benefits will definitely choose to shop repeatedly with you.

- **Customer Data:** It enables a business owner to capture customer information and track purchase history. A retailer can design the marketing strategy keeping those data in his mind. This also helps him in differentiating his customers for these special offers.

- **Cross selling opportunities:** Customer loyalty cards guarantee cross selling opportunities for a retailer. When the business owner has every detail of his customer's buying patterns, he can surely persuade him to buy something costlier.

- **Enhance brand image:** A customer loyalty card enhances brand image and also reinforces brand position. Loyalty cards in customers' wallets are a constant reminder of the brand.

- **Enhances your corporate image and brand recall:** These loyalty cards also work towards brand recall. Cardholders see your logo and brand every time they use their cards, and recall it more often.

- **Increase communication:** Cardholders receive a monthly statement containing promotions, news, and information about the company's new products. This provides a direct communication channel between the company and its customers that would otherwise be too expensive to operate.

- **Co-branding opportunities:** A loyalty card also brings the opportunity of tying up with a suitable partner whose target customer is from the same social rung, for example, the First Citizen Citibank MasterCard, a co-branded card launched by Shoppers' Stop in association with Citibank and MasterCard.

A retail establishment or a retail group may issue a loyalty card to a consumer who can then use it as a form of identification when dealing with that retailer. By presenting the card, the purchaser is typically entitled to either a discount on the current purchase, or an allotment of points that can be used for future purchases. Hence, the card is the visible means of implementing a type of what economists call a two-part tariff.

The card issuer requests or requires customers seeking the issuance of a loyalty card to provide a usually minimal amount of identifying or demographic data, such as name and address. Application forms usually entail agreements by the store concerning customer privacy, typically non-disclosure (by the store) of non-aggregate data about customers. The store as one might expect uses aggregate data internally (and sometimes externally) as part of its marketing research.

Where a customer has provided sufficient identifying information, the loyalty card may also be used to access such information to expedite verification during receipt of cheques or dispensing of medical prescription preparations, or for other membership privileges (e.g., access to a club lounge in airports, using a frequent flyer card).

Critics see the lower prices and rewards as bribes to manipulate customer loyalty and purchasing decisions, or as a case of infrequent-spenders subsidizing frequent-spenders. Others worry about the commercial use of the personal data collected as part of the programmes. It is also possible that consumer purchases are tracked and analyzed toward more efficient marketing and advertising (in fact the very raison d'etre of the loyalty card). There also remains the possibility that law enforcement agencies could be granted access to the stored information during an investigation of a customer's activities.

A loyal customer leads to repeat customers and builds brand value, so it should be a surprise to find that loyalty programs are on the top of most retailers' strategy map than any other single marketing program, the commercial benefits of loyal customers are well known by brand managers. With all the different companies offering new strategies in loyalty programs it is very important not to lose sight of the basic strategy behind implementing the loyalty program.

15.5 Consumer Profiling

All business are not born equal your business has its own unique process and your customers are different from your competitors in some stubble way. The goal when you are segregating customers is to identify a great customer from your average customer. Look at key indicators they may be in the form of which locality the customer's are coming from what does your customer do, what category of items he purchases, etc. For Ex if you find a huge segment of your customers coming from a particular locality you can work with your advertising strategy to find out what works for that locality. For ex if customers buy the Xbox from you it does result in a repeat customer since he is going to come back for games and you can target him based on his preference, the strategy of any program should be to identify the customer groups.

Define Your Customer Groups

Each customer group behaves differently spend time to examine each of these groups define elements which make up this group. Your loyalty Strategy should be based on addressing the requirements of each group understand that Loyalty is an emotional experience so spend time with defining the profile of the group Try to keep larger groups unless you have a lot of resources who can spend time in working with each of the groups.

Set Goals for Each Segment

Once you have defined your loyalty customer groups set goals to achieve for each of the groups make sure that your low level strategy to achieve your goals fits within the overall brand image. The goals and targets should be a measurable; it could be higher average billing, more customer referrals, and more frequent visits, growing the group or trying to bring about certain behaviour in the group. Document all the work you do so that you know what works for one group and what does not work priorities based on success and return on investment, what works for one group may not work for another group. Most Customer strategy fails because they are one sided and ignore the customer.

Develop loyalty strategies to accomplish each objective, the strategy for each group could look very different don't worry about it as long as it does not dilute the brand image or your high level strategy.

Concluding

At this point you know what works and what does not work you will have a set of strategies, which works. If the methods are consistent, then you could impose an overall strategy that is a common set of the strategies that worked for different groups. But most times it is very difficult to see what works for all groups so you have a series of lexical analysis that accommodates the majority of your loyal customers. For a successful loyalty program takes a lot of iteration and research.

15.6 Popular Loyalty Programmes in India

The Inner Circle (Lifestyle)

The Inner Circle is Lifestyle's exclusive Membership Club, where privileges are the order of the day. Established in 2001, 'The Inner Circle' currently has an active member base of 5.5 lac members spread across all the states that Lifestyle is present in. By virtue of membership one can gain, Reward points for every purchase made with Lifestyle, Periodic special offers/discounts from in-store brands, Invites for exclusive preview of merchandise and off Sale, Personalized updates & information on in-store promotions, marketing events, new arrivals, launch of merchandise/product, etc. One can discover that the privileges extend beyond the Lifestyle gates impacting various aspects of your life. Enjoy exclusive additional discounts from various eat outs/restaurants in India, pubs, discothèques, hospitals, health clubs/gym/theme parks, hotels, travel and entertainment.

The First Citizen (Shopper's Stop)

Shoppers' Stop's customer loyalty program is called The First Citizen. The program offers its members an opportunity to collect points and avail of innumerable special benefits. Currently, Shoppers' Stop has a database  of over 23 lakh members who contribute to nearly 72% of the total sales of Shoppers' Stop.

Club west (Westside)

Club West, is a customer loyalty programme of Westside launched in May 2001. The 30,000-  plus members of this club get rebates at restaurants and on holiday packages from the Taj Group of Hotels, home delivery of alterations, and special shopping hours on the first day of any discount sales event organized by the chain. Westside's Club West is a tier 2 rewards scheme – Classic card and Gold membership. One can become a Classic card member either by shopping for Rs. 2000 and more or by paying Rs. 150. In order to become a Gold card member, one needs to shop for Rs. 5000. Between the two cards, the percentage of reward points differs. For every purchase of Rs. 50, the Classic card member earns a point, while the Gold card member earns a point for every purchase of Rs. 40.

Green Card (Pantaloons)

 Green card is the loyalty card of pantaloon retails. Its benefits include discounts on every purchase, exclusive shopping days, regular updates about new products through mails, catalogues sms. Extended exchange periods, complimentary alteration etc are also part of the deal.

I – mint

I-mint, the multi-brand consumer rewards programme pioneered by Loyalty Solutions and Research Ltd. I-mint has 2,500 partners including HPCL, Airtel, Makemytrip and Music World, covering 3,000 outlets. The I-mint loyalty programme has over 10 million members.

Retailing Post Pandemic across the World

A familiar shopping experience can put your customers' very real fears of a **pandemic** at ease. **Retailers** will need to create or re-create shopping environments that emphasize cleanliness, and support a more distanced way of shopping. Actions can include: enhanced e-commerce and pick-up-in-store options. Metro Cash & Carry for example offer you option of forwarding your shopping List on its dedicated WhatsApp number and you can just pay online and pick up your stuff thus avoiding queue for entry, picking your sanitized trolley and risk of being in a crowd and searching for your shopping list.

The National Retail Federation (NRF) head quartered in USA has created a protocol for reopening of retail stores.

Operation Open Doors (Courtesy NRF)

NRF's Operation Open Doors provides a roadmap for safely reopening stores.

Developed with input from hundreds of retailers brought together by NRF, the initiative provides operational guidelines and considerations in four areas: health and safety, people and personnel, logistics and supply chain, and litigation and liability.

As retailers slowly reopen across the country, the single most critical thing to remember about post-COVID-19 retail design is this: Stay flexible. Many design changes retailers make today could very well need to change again, within a matter of months. NRF reached out to six retail design specialists and consultants in markets across the country for their thoughts on how retail design might change. Here are their key suggestions.

Think Strategically

Stay flexible. Flexibility in near-term retail design — not change for the sake of change — might be critical, says Mara Devitt, senior partner at retail design firm **McMillan Doolittle**. "The rules will change again, and expectations will change — which has always been the case in retail." Flexible design means that instead of making permanent bricks-and-mortar changes, allow for things like store layout to be easily modified when consumer demand takes a different turn.

Bolster Online Sales Efforts

Online sales will become an increasingly large component of overall sales. The pandemic has served to boost this ongoing trend into a much higher gear, says Candace Corlett, president of **WSL Strategic Retail.** "Those who are not strong in online retail will have to ramp up quickly," she says. Mass merchants will have to get even better at online sales.

Even before consumers walk into the store, it's critical to build trust in terms of safety, cleanliness and maintenance.

Communicate Safety Efforts

Even before consumers walk into the store, it's critical to build trust in terms of safety, cleanliness and maintenance, Devitt says. It's all about letting consumers know before they come in the store what to expect once they're inside of the store. Whether it's showing them how properly keep distance while standing in line or updates on a safer checkout process, it's incumbent on retailers to make changes or new rules perfectly clear.

Become a Place of Purpose

Instead of retailers presenting themselves as places to browse, get entertained and discover impulse items, some will want to become more purposeful places where consumers specifically go to get an item or two — and get out, says Kirthi Kalyanam, executive director of the Retail Management Institute at Santa Clara University.

Consider the Customer Experience

Revamp "treasure hunt" shopping

Many shoppers love "treasure hunt" shopping at off-price chains. But Devitt says there could be simple ways for retailers to make that treasure hunt more comfortable in a post-pandemic world. For example, clearance bins could be transparent; customers could rummage through them with disinfected devices or with gloves. Gloves could also be provided for customers browsing racks.

Encourage shopping appointments

Imagine new spaces within stores for those who previously booked shopping appointments online. Shoppers might enter a especially reserved space where a salesperson listens to their needs and then collects — and presents — the things they want, Devitt says. The isolated space lets shoppers keep their distance from other shoppers while receiving very personal care from a salesperson.

Limit occupancy levels

Store occupancy levels could be the most critical — but most problematic — issue retailers' face going forward. The issue might vary significantly from market to market and from one city to the next, says Doug Stephens, founder of consulting firm Retail Prophet. Some retailers might need to consider evolving the role of the store greeter to someone who counts — and limits — the number of customers in the store, says Jody Wasbro, senior vice president of strategy and experience design at WD Partners.

Create transition space at the entrance

This might be the single most common post-COVID-19 design change to most retailers. "Think of it as a decompression space," Devitt says. It can function as an educational check-in area where shoppers are informed of what safety actions the store is taking and what safety actions are expected of them. Most stores will try to smoothly link their own brand's iconic branding elements to the transition area, she says, so it all feels unique.

Redo sampling

Retailers — particularly cosmetics retailers — that rely on some form of product sampling might want to redo the physical setup and the sampling methodology, Devitt says. Instead of dipping into a previously opened jar of face cream, for example, cosmetics samples will need to be single-use. Some forms of digital makeup sampling done online with imagery could gain traction. Vichy Cosmetics use to dispense sampling in sachets since last 15 years back when they launched it.

As more customers request product pickup options, retailers will want to vastly improve the experience.

Create a better pickup experience

As more customers request product pickup options, Wasbro says retailers will want to vastly improve the experience. Pickup should be appointment-only to eliminate long lines; in areas of the country that are prone to adverse weather, retailers might want to cover pickup areas for driver comfort.

Avoid congestion at checkout

What if checkout could be eliminated entirely, such as at Amazon Go stores? Or perhaps the same folks who formerly worked at checkout could be redeployed to keep the store looking pristine, healthy and safe, Corlett says. Where this isn't practical, checkout stations should be closely monitored for safe customer spacing and constant cleaning.

Focus on Facilities

Create clean employee areas

Employee areas will be less about lockers to store coats, and more about overall employee wellness. Some retailers might want to consider providing employees with clean, sanitized uniforms each day for work. A key part of this tactic is communicating these moves to customers.

Rethink spatial requirements

For customer comfort, the personal space required between shoppers in checkout areas may be up to five times greater than it used to be, says Jay Baptista, senior principal at retail design specialist Stantec.

Use different materials

Retailers will want to present smoother surfaces that broadly discourage bacteria and live viruses, Wasbro says. That could mean fewer wood surfaces and even different paint textures that are smoother.

Eliminate handles and knobs

In a world where customers are going to feel increasingly reluctant to touch anything, Stephens says handles and knobs are among the easiest things to eliminate. Doors can be made to push open without touching handles — or open automatically with the wave of a hand.

Show carts being sanitized

Retailers should make a very public display of how they sanitize their carts, Wasbro says. Carts can no longer simply be stacked outdoors. They should be fully sanitized inside by a designated employee or, perhaps in the future, with some form of UV lighting or some sort of mechanized disinfectant system.

Consider germ-free shelving

Retailers might want to investigate what types of shelving are most commonly used in healthcare environments like hospitals and doctors' offices, Baptista says, and decide if that translates into a healthier retail environment.

Create one-way aisles

In order to eliminate bottlenecks and speed up the shopping process, Stephens says some retailers might want to consider creating one-way aisles.

Consumers who are concerned about high-touch areas might view kiosks through an entirely different lens going forward.

Eliminate kiosks

For years, major restaurant retailers in particular have created kiosks to assist customers in ordering more quickly and reducing long lines at the cashier. But consumers who are concerned about high-touch areas might view kiosks through an entirely different lens going forward. Retailers might want to think carefully before adding more kiosks and instead facilitate more contactless ways to order, such as via cell phone. "Why touch something that tens of thousands of others have touched before you?" Stephens says.

Revamp fitting rooms

Making fitting rooms sterile will be a major challenge, particularly since many are carpeted. All clothing, however, would need to be sealed — then publicly sanitized and sealed again after it's been tried on. "This will require a major reset," Kalyanam says.

Keep products in storage

Think of this as a flashback to the full-service shoe store, where there are a very limited number of items on display and a salesperson goes to the storage area and brings customers the exact products they want to try on. "The whole try-on experience will be reimagined," Devitt says. Once items are tried on, there will need to be an immediate sanitation process that customers can see.

Eliminate impulse displays

To keep checkout quick, simple and sanitary, Wasbro says retailers might want to remove the impulse purchases routinely stacked at checkout counters.

No matter what, retailers should never make any physical changes chain-wide without first testing it out in several stores, Devitt says. Also, run the changes by local regulators first, just to make sure there are no surprises. And while design changes are being trailed, she says, don't forget to specifically ask employees and customers for their feedback.

Retail Terminology

A

Add on sales – Add-on sales is the promotion of additional products or services to a customer at the time of purchase.

Administration – Facilitation, Administration Department in Retail facilitates all the other department in areas of security, housekeeping, stationary, office requirements etc.

Advertisement – Advertising is a form of communication used to persuade an audience (viewers, readers or listeners) to take some action with respect to products, ideas, or services. Most commonly, the desired result is to drive consumer behaviour with respect to a commercial offering, although political and ideological advertising is also common. Advertising messages are usually paid for by sponsors and viewed via various traditional media; including mass media such as newspaper, magazines, television commercial, radio advertisement, outdoor advertising or direct mail; or new media such as websites and text messages.

Aisle – An aisle is, in general, a space for walking with rows of seats on either side or with rows of seats on one side and a wall on the other. Aisles can be seen in airplanes. Aisles can also be seen in shops, warehouses, and factories, where rather than seats they have shelving to either side. In warehouses and factories aisles may consist of storage pallets and in factories aisles may separate work areas. In health clubs, exercise equipment normally is arranged in aisles.

Alteration – Alteration is the change. Change that does not affect the basic character or structure of the thing it is applied to. In retail alteration word is used for the apparel department. When garments are modified for the customers according to his size. For an example, the length of a trouser is shorten according to customer's length is an alteration.

Ambience, Atmosphere – A particular environment or surrounding or condition of the place. For an example friendly youthful ambience in Café Coffee Day and a serious, elegant ambience in Van Heusen show rooms.

Apparel – Apparel is the second name of garments and clothes.

ARS – Automatic Replenishment System.

Assortment – A collection or group of various things or sorts, assorting means distribution and classification.

Audit – Audit is an evaluation of a person, organization, system, process, enterprise, project or product. The term most commonly refers to audits in accounting, but similar concepts also exist in project management, quality management, and energy conservation.

Autumn Winter Season – Fashion products are divided in to two seasons. One of it is Autumn Winter where woolen, warm, full sleeves & full neck, dark coloured clothes come in fashion. In case of Indian fashion industry the duration for autumn winter season August to December.

B

B2B – B2B means Business to Business. Business-to-business describes commerce transactions between businesses, such as between a manufacturer and a wholesaler, or between a wholesaler and a retailer.

B2C – B2C means Business to Consumer. It describes activities of businesses serving end consumers with products and/or services. An example of a B2C transaction would be a person buying a pair of shoes from a retailer.

Bakery – A bakery (also called baker's shop or baking house) is an establishment which produces or/and sells baked goods from an oven such as: bread, pies, bagels, pastries, cakes and cupcakes, biscuits, cookies, crackers, muffins, rolls, pretzels, doughnuts, and other items prepared by bakers. Some retail bakeries and many new bakeries are also cafés, serving coffee and tea to customers who wish to consume the baked goods on the premises.

Barcode – A unique identifier for an inventory item or for a particular colour/size combination for an item. A barcode may be printed in machine readable format using one of a number of common symbolises, such as UPC-A, Code 39, etc.

Bargain – Bargain means the process whereby buyer and seller agree the price of goods or services. It is an agreement to exchange goods at a price. Such an agreement where one of the parties thinks the price is very favourable.

Barter System – Barter System is that system in which goods are exchanged for goods. In ancient times when money was not invented trade as a whole was on barter system.

Bay – Bay is a partition of the wall for the display of products. Generally this partition is decided as per company's standards. It can be 3 feet or 4 feet.

Bazaar – Bazaar is a Hindi word for a permanent merchandising area, marketplace, or street of shops where goods and services are exchanged or sold.

Beverages – Beverage is any liquid suitable for drinking.

Bin – Represents a physical place to store inventory. Bins are subdivisions of a location and are used to locate items. Generally, bins refer to physical rows/shelves or to actual bins.

Bottom Line – Refers to a company's net earnings, net income or earnings per share (EPS). Bottom line also refers to any actions that may increase/decrease net earnings or a company's overall profit. A company that is growing its net earnings or reducing its costs is said to be "improving its bottom line".

Brand – Brand is a name, term, design, symbol, or any other feature that identifies one seller's good or service as distinct from those of other sellers. The legal term for brand is trademark. A brand may identify one item, a family of items, or all items of that seller.

Browsing – Browsing in Retail is searching and analysing the merchandise in the store.

Buyer – An executive who is responsible for selecting, pricing, and purchasing merchandise. In many companies, the term "buyer" designates a department manager, whose responsibilities include, but are broader than, the purchasing function.

C

Capex – Capital expenditures (CAPEX or capex) are expenditures creating future benefits. A capital expenditure is incurred when a business spends money either to buy fixed assets or to add to the value of an existing fixed asset with a useful life that extends beyond the taxable year. Capex are used by a company to acquire or upgrade physical assets such as equipment, property, or industrial buildings.

Cash Counter – Cash Counter is the Counter near the exit of the store where billing is done.

Cash Till – Cash Till is the second name of cash counter in retail.

Casual Clothes – Casual is the dress code that emphasizes comfort and personal expression over presentation and uniformity. Jeans comes under casual wear.

Catchment Area – Catchment area is the area and population from which a facility or region attracts visitors or customers.

Category – A classification assigned to retail items. Categories are useful for grouping similar items for pricing and reporting purposes.

Category adjacencies – Category Adjacencies in retail means to decide which category will remain beside which category.

Category Killer Stores – Category killers are small specialty stores which have expanded to offer a full range of a particular category. They are called category killers as they specialize in their fields.

Chiller – A chiller is a machine that works as a freezer for some of the bakery products in the store.

Client – Client is a customer who comes to buy a service. For an example, person who comes to a hair cutting saloon for hair cut is called a client. A person who seeks for a lawyer service is also called a client.

Closing the sale – Closing is the final step of transaction in sale. In sales, it is used more generally to mean achievement of the desired outcome, which may be an exchange of money or acquiring a signature.

Colour Blocking – Colour Blocking is the process of arranging products in a particular flow which makes it look visually good and easy for browse.

Commerce – While business refers to the value-creating activities of an organization for profit, commerce means the whole system of an economy that constitutes an environment for business. The system includes legal, economic, political, social, cultural, and technological systems that are in operation in any company.

Commodities – Commodity refers to the product.

Competitor – Any person or entity which is a rival against another. In business, a company in the same industry or a similar industry which offers a similar product or service is competitor.

Consumer – Consumer is the one who consumes or uses the product. For an example, a servant who goes to buy bread from the market is the customer but the master who is going to eat that bread is a consumer.

Coordinate clothes – Coordinate clothes are generally seen in kids wear section. These are the clothes with pre-defined pair of top and bottom.

Crates – Crates in retail is a basket like container which is used to display the vegetables and fruits.

Credit Note – Credit note is a commercial document issued by a seller to a buyer. The seller usually issues a Credit Memo for the same or lower amount than the invoice, and then repays the money to the buyer or sets it off against a balance due from other transactions.

CRM – Customer Relationship Management is a widely-implemented strategy for managing a company's interactions with customers, clients and sales prospects. The overall goals are to find, attract, and win new clients, nurture and retain those the company already has, entice former clients back into the fold, and reduce the costs of marketing and client service.

Cross Merchandising – Cross merchandising is the practice of marketing, or displaying products from different categories (or store departments) together, in order to generate additional revenue, known sometimes as add-on sales, or incremental purchase.

Cross Selling – Cross Selling is the practice adopted by the sales representative to sell the related product. If a customer buys a shirt, selling him a matching tie will be an example of cross selling.

CSA – Customer Sales Associate, CSA is a sales representative who is directly involved with the customers for selling the products and services. They help customers in finding out the needed product, explain them the use, and guide them for other store products.

CSD – Customer Service Desk, CSD is the place in the store where customers resolve their problems. CSD is engaged in activities like exchanging products, issuing credit notes, alterations, gift wrapping, complaints handling, announcements, lost and found and other service related activities.

Currency – In economics, currency refers to a generally accepted medium of exchange. These are usually the coins and banknotes of a particular government, which comprise the physical aspects of a nation's money supply.

Customer – An individual or organization that purchases goods and services from your company.

Customer Delight – Customer Delight means more than just feeling great about a product or service. Customer delight means the customer demonstrates high return and recommends rate behaviour. Delighted customers will tell six to nine people out of ten about their satisfaction experience, and it is guaranteed that some of these folks will also tell others.

Customer Flow – Customer flow is the direction where all the customers are moving. In retail, the way in which customers move across the store is customers flow.

Customer Satisfaction – Customer satisfaction, a term frequently used in marketing, is a measure of how products and services supplied by a company meet or surpass customer expectation. Customer satisfaction is defined as "the number of customers, or percentage of total customers, whose reported experience with a firm, its products, or its services (ratings) exceeds specified satisfaction goals.

D

D bar – D bar is the type of fixture. It is an iron rod which retailers use for side hanging of the clothes.

Data Base – A database is an organized collection of data for one or more purposes, usually in digital form. The term "database" refers both to the way its users view it, and to the logical and physical materialization of its data, content, in files, computer memory, and computer data storage.

DC (Distribution center) – A distribution center for a set of products is a warehouse or other specialized building, often with refrigeration or air conditioning, which is stocked with products (goods) to be redistributed to retailers, to wholesalers, or directly to consumers.

Deal – In retail deal is a term used for any offer or discount schemes.

Demographic factors – Demography is the statistical study of human population. It encompasses the study of the size, structure and distribution of these populations, and spatial and/or temporal changes in them in response to birth, migration, aging and death.

Departmental Stores – A department store is a retail establishment which satisfies a wide range of the consumer's personal and residential durable goods product needs; and at the same time offering the consumer a choice of multiple merchandise lines, at variable price points, in all product categories. Department stores usually sell products including apparel, furniture, home appliances, electronics, and additionally select other lines of products such as paint, hardware, toiletries, cosmetics, photographic equipment, jewellery, toys, and sporting goods.

Discount Stores – These stores represent a reduction in the price of an item.

Dispatch – To dispatch is to send things to a specific location.

Display – Display is the presentation of the products in a way to attract customers towards it.

Distribution – Distribution is the movement of goods and services from the source through a distribution channel, right up to the final customer, consumer, or user, and the movement of payment in the opposite direction, right up to the original producer or supplier.

Drums – In retail, drums are cylindrical shaped fixtures to stock the staple food like rice, wheat and other cereals and pulses.

Dunnage – Dunnage is the lower platform to display heavy products in the store like 5 and 10 kg detergent packets.

Durable goods – In economics, a durable good or a hard good is a good that does not quickly wear out, or more specifically, one that yields utility over time rather than being completely consumed in one use. Items like bricks or jewelry could be considered perfectly durable goods, because they should theoretically never wear out. Highly durable goods such as refrigerators, cars, or mobile phones usually continue to be useful for three or more years of use, so durable goods are typically characterized by long periods between successive purchases.

E

EBO – Exclusive Brand Outlet. This term is referred to the stores where only one brand is available. All the products like clothes, accessories, home linen etc are of the same brand only.

Economies of scale – Economies of scale, in microeconomics, refer to the cost advantages that a business obtains due to expansion. "Economies of scale" is a long run concept and refers to reductions in unit cost as the size of a facility and the usage levels of other inputs increase.

EDC (Electronic Draft Capture) – An automatic method of authorizing, balancing, and settling credit card transactions entered in your retail software package.

Electronic Media – Electronic Media is the electronic channel through which companies communicate about their products and promotions to the customers. Television, radio, internet etc. are examples of electronic media.

End Caps – The end pieces of display units typically used to display promotional items or featured items.

ERP System – Enterprise Resource Planning integrates internal and external management information across an entire organization, embracing finance/accounting, manufacturing, sales and service, customer relationship management, etc. ERP systems automate this activity with an integrated software application. Its purpose is to facilitate the flow of information between all business functions inside the boundaries of the organization and manage the connections to outside stakeholders.

ERT (Emergency Response Technique) – ERT includes fire safety, electrical safety, floor safety, accident reporting, and first aid techniques.

E-tailers – Merchants who sell retail goods or services through the Internet. Related terms: internet retail, retail ecommerce, online retailing, ecommerce, e-retail, e-tail, and e-tailing.

Ethnic Wear – Ethnic wear refers to the India dress like kurtha, pyjama, sarees and other Indian traditional dresses.

Evolution – Evolution is the change over time in one or more inherited traits found in populations of organisms.

Experience Design – Experience design is the team in retail which designs the experience of the customers. This team is also known as Visual Merchandising team. It works towards attractive displays, designing the store atmosphere and deciding on merchandise presentation.

Expiry date/Shelf life – Shelf life is the length of time that food, drink, medicine, chemicals, and many other perishable items are given before they are considered unsuitable for sale, use, or consumption. In some regions, a best before, use by or freshness date is required on packaged perishable foods.

F

F & B – Food & Beverages.

F & V – Fruits & Vegetables.

F & V Lounger – Lounger is a slant fixture made of iron to display the crates or baskets for fruits and vegetables.

Fashion Accessories – Fashion accessories are decorative items that supplement and complement clothes, such as jewellery, gloves, handbags, hats, belts, scarves, watches, sunglasses, pins, stockings, bow ties, leg warmers, leggings, neckties, suspenders, tights, handbags, hats etc.

Façade – façade is generally one side of the exterior of a building, especially the front, but also sometimes the sides and rear. The word comes from the French language, literally meaning "frontage" or "face".

Factory Outlet – Factory outlet is a store where products are available at cheaper rates than the exclusive store of the same brand. Factory outlets keep products which are old or with minor defects which are sold for cheaper rates than the exclusive store.

Fashion – Fashion, a general term for a currently popular style or practice, especially in clothing, foot wear or accessories. Fashion references to anything that is the current trend in look and dress up of a person.

Fixtures – In retail, fixture means all the different type of furniture in the store where we display the products.

Flyers/insert/leaflet – Flyer or an insert is the small paper with being inserted in daily newspaper or distributed in schools and colleges and other public places for advertisement.

FMCG – Fast Moving Consumer Goods, these are the products that are sold quickly and at relatively low cost. Examples include non-durable goods such as soft drinks, toiletries, and grocery items.

Focal Point – Focal point is a term used for Visual Merchandising. A display which represents some story with the group of mannequins and other decorative and supportive elements displayed at one place is called a focal point.

Footfalls – In retail, footfall refers to the number of entries happened in a day in a store. Number of footfalls are not necessarily equal to number of bills happened because many people who come to the store, do not necessarily make a purchase.

Formal wear – Formal wear and formal dress are the general terms for clothing suitable for formal social events, such as a wedding, formal garden party or dinner, debutante cotillion, dance, or race.

Four Way Browser – Four Way Browser is one of the type of fixtures used for displaying the garments in the store. Garments are hanged on the four way browser. The name depicts the fixtures design. It has four iron hands in four directions for display.

Frisking – Frisking is a search of a person's outer clothing wherein a person runs his or her hands along the outer garments to detect any concealed weapons or contraband.

G

Gap Table – Gap Table refers to the three tiered table where clothes are folded and stacked.

General Merchandise – General Merchandise refers to the category which includes products like plastics, utensils, crockery, cleaning materials, gift articles and footwear. This category does not include and food or fashion products.

General Stores – General store refers to the local kirana store where daily needed things are available. It is an unorganised format of retail.

Gift Vouchers (GV) – A voucher for goods or services that is sold to one customer with the expectation that it will be redeemed by another. Generally people buy GVs of certain amount and gift it to another person instead of buying any product or gift.

Global Counting – Global Counting is the practice carried in retail stores everyday by the sales representative to physically count the number of products available in each category. By this, they come to know if the actual number of products available is differing from the system number and take necessary action.

Gondola – Gondola is the fixture used in retail stores. It is referred to the separate floor fixture which is open from all the four sides and not connected to wall.

Goods – Good is a product that can be used to satisfy some desire or need. More narrowly but commonly, a good is a tangible physical product that can be contrasted with a service which is intangible.

Greeting – Greeting means welcoming the customers with a smile and good wishes.

Grooming – Personal grooming is the art of cleaning, grooming, and maintaining parts of the body. Clean ironed clothes, nicely combed hair, trimmed nails etc. are the part of grooming.

H

Hard Tag – Hard tag is the security tag placed on all the products so that no one can carry it out without removing the tag and tag can be removed only by the company people after billing the product. This tag is mostly put on the garments.

Heaper – Heaper is a kind of display done in the stores. This display is generally for the heavy products which are arranged neatly on a lower platform on the ground one upon another.

Hoardings – Hoardings are the advertisement boards hired by the companies on the public roads.

House Keeping – House Keeping is the team which takes care of the cleanliness of the store, toilets and store rooms.

Human Resource – Human resource is the support team in the stores which takes care of the recruitments, appraisals, welfare of the employees and also other company formalities related to employees.

Hyper Market – a hypermarket is a superstore combining a supermarket and a department store. The result is an expansive retail facility carrying a wide range of products under one roof, including full groceries lines and general merchandise. In theory, hypermarkets allow customers to satisfy all their routine shopping needs in one trip.

I

Impulse or Unplanned purchase – Impulse or unplanned purchase refers to the instant action taken by customers to purchase some product in a store. Sometimes customers get attracted to a product due to its display, packaging or a price and make an unplanned purchase.

Income Tax – An income tax is a tax levied on the income of individuals or businesses. The "tax net" refers to the types of payment that are taxed, which included personal earnings (wages), capital gains, and business income.

Infant – An infant or baby is the very young offspring of humans. A newborn is an infant who is within hours, days, or up to a few weeks from birth.

Inventory – Merchandise on-hand for sale to customers in the ordinary course of business. The raw materials, work-in-process goods and completely finished goods that are considered to be the portion of a business's assets which are ready or will be ready for sale.

Investment – Investment is putting money into something with the expectation of gain that upon thorough analysis has a high degree of security of principle, as well as security of return, within an expected period of time.

K

Kirana stores, provision store, mom &pop store – This is a small petty store in a local area. It is the most prevalent form of retail in India which is called as an unorganised retail. These stores generally serve in the categories of grocery and food.

Known Loss – Known loss is the loss of stock identified as being unfit to sell to customers. This loss is known to the store. It cannot always be a financial loss to the store. Some of the examples are expired goods, damaged goods etc.

L

Latent Need – Latent need is the hidden need in customers. Sales Representative have to develop he skill of finding out the latent needs of the customers. Sometimes customer doesn't know his need but if prompted by sales representative, he may end up buying that product.

Loss – Loss is a negative difference between retail price and cost of production. Loss happens when selling price is less than the cost price.

Loyalty – Commitment to a particular store or brand.

M

Maintenance – maintenance is the department in a retail store which takes care of technical aspects in the store like the generator, ACs, electrical equipment, fire equipment, CCTVs in the store etc.

Malls – Mall is one or more buildings forming a complex of shops representing merchandisers, with interconnecting walkways enabling visitors to easily walk from unit to unit, along with a parking area — a modern, indoor version of the traditional marketplace.

Mannequin – A mannequin, also called a dummy, lay figure or dress form, is an often articulated doll used by artists, tailors, dressmakers, and others especially to display or fit clothing.

Margins – The difference between the cost of an item and its price.

Mark up – Upward revision of the original retail price, resulting in a price higher than the original price.

Markdown – A reduction in the original retail price, primarily taken for clearance of broken merchandise, prior stock, or to meet competitor's pricing.

Marketing – Marketing is the process used to determine what products or services may be of interest to customers, and the strategy to use in sales, communications and business development.

MBO – Multi Brand Outlet. MBO is a store where various brands will be sold under one roof.

MBQ – Minimum Base Quantity. It refers to smallest volume that can be handled and displayed in the store.

Merchandising – Buying and selling of goods.

Modern Market – Modern market in retail refers to the organised retailing with busy shopping malls, multi storied malls and huge complexes that offer a large variety of products in terms of quality, value for money and makes shopping a memorable experience.

MRP (Maximum Retail Price) – Typically, the highest price at which an item is sold.

N

Nesting Table – One set of three or four tables that are graduated in size so that they may be stacked on top of another.

Needs – A need is something that is necessary for organisms to live a healthy life. Needs can be objective and physical, such as food, or they can be subjective and psychological, such as the need for self-esteem.

Non Food – being something that is not food but is sold in a supermarket, as housewares or stationery.

O

Objection – Dissatisfaction of customer on a product or service.

Offers – price lesser than MRP.

Operations – A team directly deals with the final customer in selling or marketing the product or the sales team in retail.

Organised Retail – Organized retailing comprises mainly of modern retailing with busy shopping malls, multi storied malls and huge complexes that offer a large variety of products in terms of quality, value for money and makes shopping a memorable experience.

P

Packaging – Packaging refers to the container or wrapper that holds a product or group of products.

Packers – One that packs: a packer of boxes in a warehouse or at the cash counters.

Pallets – A portable platform used for displaying heavy goods in a heap form on floor. Especially in Food packets like wheat flour.

Passage – Path between the rack or gondola or department in the store for the easy browsing.

Performance Appraisal – A performance appraisal, employee appraisal, performance review, or career development discussion is a method by which the job performance of an employee is evaluated. Generally in terms of quality, quantity, cost, and time. Typically by the corresponding manager or supervisor.

Perishable – Article that can lose its usefulness and value if not appropriately stored or transported, or if not utilized within certain period like fruits and vegetables.

Personal selling – Personal Selling is the method of selling goods and services by going to each and every customers, making them understand the benefit and then selling the product. Generally for personal selling, a sales representative goes to the houses and offices of a customer and makes sells.

Petty cash – small amounts of cash kept on hand in a business (sum of money given to the cashier before he starts the billing).

Pilferage – Reduction in inventory caused by employees or customers (shrinkage). It is the act or practice of stealing small quantities or articles.

Planogram – Schematic drawings of retail store fixtures that illustrate product placement.

Podium – A platform used for conducting activities or promotions in the store.

Policies – a course of action adopted and pursued by a retailer to sell the product n services to the customer.

POS – The physical location at which goods or services are sold to customers. It is also called point of purchase (POP).

POS System – A computerized system made up of retail software and point of sale hardware. Retail POS systems expedite point of sale checkouts, track merchandise performance, reorder items, identify sales trends, enable buyers to make better merchandising decisions, track customers and monitor loyalty, and report on historical sales activity.

Positioning – The creation of an image for a product or service in the minds of customers, both specifically to that item and in relation to competitive offerings.

Price Range – Different prices between the least price and highest price. The different prices of a product to meet the all sections of customers.

Price – The amount a customer would pay to buy a particular item from you, or what a customer actually paid for an item.

Primary Activities – a stage of conversation of a raw material to a final good.

Prime Hours – The maximum number of customers' walk-in or peak hours in shopping.

Print and Production – Print & production is a team which is part of visual merchandising team. This team works on the entire in store communications.

Print Media – The industry associated with the printing and distribution of news through newspapers and magazines.

Private label – Private label is the collection of products owned by the retailer. It is his private brand which can be sold only in his stores across India.

Profit – The positive gain from an investment or business operation after subtracting for all expenses. It is an opposite of loss.

Promotions – A special item price available for a limited period of time.

Psychographic Factors – Psychographic factors are customer's traits according to their psychology and lifestyle habits.

Q

Queue Manager – Queue manager is around 4 ft. vertical iron rod with stretchable bands on both the sides which can be used for managing the queue of customers while billing.

R

Rack – rack is a shelf where products are being displayed.

Rationing – Fair Price shops, public distribution system (PDS).

Raw Material – Goods that are unfinished that are used to produce goods that are finished.

Recruitment – Recruitment is the procedure to hire new people for the company Recruitments are part of HR team.

Refilling – Refilling is the process of filling again by supplying what has been sold.

Replenishment – The process of filling the shelves in store.

Retail – An individual or company that sells goods and services directly to the consumer.

Retail Format – Retail Format refers to the nature of seller and its product assortment.

RFID – Radio-frequency identification – Radio frequency identification (RFID) is a generic term that is used to describe a system that transmits the identity (in the form of a unique serial number) of an object or person wirelessly, using radio waves. It's grouped under the broad category of automatic identification technologies.

S

Sales Representative – salesperson: a person employed to represent a business and to sell its merchandise (as to customers in a store or to customers who are visited).

Sales tax – a tax based on the cost of the item purchased and collected directly from the buyer.

Scanner – A device to capture the product information instantly.

Schemes – a specific proposal to sell the product.

SCM – Supply chain management (SCM) is the management of a network of interconnected businesses involved in the ultimate provision of product and service packages required by end customer.

Seal – Seal in the context of retail is a paper stuck on the lock of the store with the signature of security and manager while closing the store for the day.

Secondary Activities – Activities where natural resources are made or manufactured in factories into goods.

Security – a support team in a store which takes care of security factors related to store.

Security Tag – Security tag is the tag on all the products to avoid theft and shop lifting. If somebody carries product outside the store without billing then these tag get detected by the machine at the exit of the store and it starts beeping so that security can sense the theft and take required actions.

Segment – A segment is a sub-set of a market made up of people or organizations with one or more characteristics that cause them to demand similar product and/or services based on qualities of those products such as price or function.

SEL – Shelf edge label, it is a label with product barcode and price, stuck on the shelf.

Selling – is offering to exchange something of value for something else or the last step in the chain of commerce where a buyer exchanges cash for a seller's good or service, or the activity of trying to bring this about.

Selling Skill – A developed talent or ability to sell the merchandise or to make customer happy.

Service – Service is the intangible service provided to the customers. For an example, hair cutting saloons give service to the customers.

Shelf – A flat piece of wood, plastic or glass that is attached to the wall or is part of a piece of furniture, used for display of the product.

Shandy day – Shandy day is the term used for traditional retail market in early days where one day was being decided to sell and buy the product at the outskirts of village.

Shelf Talker – Printed card or other sign attached to a store shelf to give information of the product which is displayed on that shelf.

Shop Lifting – the act of stealing goods from store is called shop lifting.

Shrinkage – The difference between actual stock and book records of stock. Shrinkage represents the aggregate of errors in stock record keeping, plus actual losses of merchandise through shoplifting, employee theft, paperwork errors, breakage, etc.

Side Hanging – Displaying of goods from above with no support from below.

Signage – A signage represents some piece of information like, price, size, and quantity location name.

SIS – Shop In Shop – SIS means a small space hired for your brand in a department store. For an example, a 1000 square feet space for Levi's brand in Bangalore Central.

Size Blocking – Size blocking is displaying the merchandise in a way that the smallest size comes first and largest size comes last while browsing.

SKU – Stock keeping unit, a number used to identify each unique item. SKUs are used in retail software to identify items.

Soft Tag – An electronic unit (device) of information used as a label or marker, used for security of purpose.

SOP – Standard Operating Process, SOP refers to the standardized rules made for the company which has to be followed across India. One of the examples of the SOP can be an Exchange policy of the store.

Specialty Stores – retail chains, which deal in specific categories and provide deep assortment in them are specialty stores.

Spring Summer Season – In fashion products retailing, the merchandise style, colours and designs are being decided according to the season. Spring Summer and Autumn winter are two seasons which are being followed in Industry. The period for Spring Summer season is January to July.

Stacking – to arrange products in a way so that they are placed one on top of another.

Staple – a chief or main item (of diet etc.). Or necessary or important, especially regarding food or commodities; "wheat is a staple crop".

Stock – supply of goods kept on hand for sale to customers by a merchant, distributor, manufacturer, etc.; inventory.

Stock Movement – Stock movement in the stores means the speed of the products getting sold. A movement of the product from the shelf to the billing.

Stock takes – Stock take is the quarterly process carried out by the stores for counting the stock physically in the store and analyzing the difference between the actual quantity and the system quantity.

Store – A physical place at which retail business is conducted.

Store Layout – Store layout describes the overall look and feel of the interior of a retail store, including the placement of fixtures and products within the store.

Store Location – A convenient place for the customer & the retailer to buy & sell the products.

Store Traffic – A customer count recorded by hour, day, week, month or holiday or the number of customers who enter a store.

Super Market – These are generally large self-service outlets, offering a variety of categories with deep assortments. They offer food, clothes, furniture, electronics, home needs etc.

Supply chain – The movement of materials as they flow from their source to the end customer. Supply Chain includes purchasing, manufacturing, warehousing, transportation, customer service; demand planning, supply planning and Supply Chain management.

Support team – The facilitating team to the sales team, It includes Marketing Team, Visual Merchandising Team, Merchandising Team, Administration team etc.

Surplus – An amount or a quantity of goods in excess of what is needed or non-movement of stock in the store.

SUSD – Shutter up and Shutter down, SUSD refers to all the activities in the store before he shutter are open and after the shutters are closed in the store.

T

Tag – A physical label attached to merchandise for sale, such as an adhesive price tag, hang tag, or butterfly tag.

Target Market – A defined group of consumers whom the retailer attempts to satisfy with their products and services.

Tertiary activities – Economic activity involving providing services and distribution or sale of a finished good.

Ticket – A transaction used for the sale or return of goods or services. It is used as another word for bill.

Ticket Size – ticket Size refers to the bill amount.

Top Line – gross sales or revenues of a company. A company that increases its revenues is said to be "growing its top line", or "generating top-line growth".

Top of the mind position (TOM) – Brands which comes first in your mind while you think of any product. For an example, Colgate occupies top of the line position in cconsumer's mind when we talk about tooth-paste category. This position can be achieved generally through advertising.

Tracking – A continuous check made to know the level of achievement in any work.

Trade – Sale of goods and services.

Traditional Market – An underdeveloped economy in which communities use primitive tools and methods to produce or to sell the commodities.

Transaction – An agreement between a buyer and a seller to exchange a product for payment or the process of buying and selling.

Transportation – movement of goods from a manufacturer to a retailer or from a retailer to a customer.

Trend – A pattern of gradual change in a condition, output, of customers' likes and preferences. For an example, switching groom boot cut pant to narrow cut pants due to change in trend of pants.

Trial Room – A small room for customers to try their new garments or costumes.

Trolley – Wheeled vehicle in which you put your shopped goods while going around the supermarket. Or a large metal basket or frame on wheels, resembling a shopping cart and used for transporting merchandise in the store or a shopping cart.

Turnover – Turnover is the revenue earned by any business.

U

Unknown Loss – Reduction in inventory caused by employees or customers (shrinkage) which cannot be identified.

Unorganised Retail – Traditional or Unorganized retail outlets are normally street markets, counter stores, kiosks and vendors, where the ownership and management rest with one person.

Up selling – Upselling is a sales technique whereby a salesperson induces the customer to purchase more expensive items, upgrades, or other add-ons in an attempt to make a more profitable sale. Or Up-sell is a marketing term for the practice of suggesting higher priced products.

V

Value Store – A customer where he gets value for his money spent on purchasing goods or a commodity.

Vending Machine – Electronic machine used to disperse a product to a consumer after certain amount of money has been put into the machine. Vending machines are commonly used to disperse beverages and snack items.

Visual Merchandising – Displaying of goods in a attractive manner to catch the attention of a customer (impulse buy) or enhancing the look of a store buying arrange of merchandise in an attractive way.

W

Walk-ins – number of customer enter to the store for purchasing.

Wall – Place used for product display or for branding.

Warehouse – A place in which goods or merchandise are stored; a storehouse or A large, usually wholesale shop or A large building where raw materials or manufactured goods may be stored before their export or distribution for sale.

Water fall – A metal handle with hooks in shape of water fall used for displaying the goods. Water fall is a slant rod fixed on the wall fixture for front hanging of the clothes.

White Goods – Heavy consumer durables such as air conditioners, refrigerators, stoves, etc., which used to be painted only in white enamel finish.

Wholesaler – A distributor or middleman who sells mainly to retailers and institutions, rather than consumers or Wholesalers means trader who purchases goods in huge quantities from manufacturers and re-sales them in small quantities. In other words, the commodities which a person or firm purchases and then it sells to retailers or consumers or to commercial firms for industrial or commercial use, such firm or individual is known as wholesalers.

Window Display – A window of a store facing onto the street; used to display merchandise for sale in the store or a technique used to attract the outside customer to walk into the store.

Preventive Guidelines for
RETAIL INDUSTRY

Approved by Indian Medical Association

Workplace Sanitization

- Ensure availability of face masks for employees coming to office
- Sanitizers to be placed in all departments in addition to reception desk
- Disinfect entire office twice a week, carry out fumigation of workplace on daily basis for first 14 days
- Disinfect frequently touched areas like reception, delivery areas and surfaces such as hand rails, door handle, push plates, telephone equipment, key boards, photocopy machines and other office equipment, toilet flush and seats at regular intervals

Cafeteria

- Conduct daily temperature screening of all cafeteria staff when they enter and exit the building
- Train office boys, kitchen helpers and canteen managers to ensure high-degree of personal hygiene and strict cleanliness
- Mandate cafeteria staff to sanitize themselves on a continuous basis and wear mask and gloves while preparing and serving food
- Introduce healthy menus for employees such as immunity-enhancing diet to build their immune system. Avoid serving any raw food such as salads
- Restrict the number of employees entering the cafeteria at one point of time to prevent gathering

Travel

- Suspend all non-essential travel and exercise strict caution in making travel plans to any region
- Put a blanket ban on all business travel unless approved by top management
- Avoid inviting vendors/contractors/customers from high risk locations/affected countries to office locations

Annexures

Annexure I - Guidelines for Preparation of 1% sodium hypochlorite solution

Product	Available chlorine	1 percent
Sodium hypochlorite – liquid bleach	3.5%	1 part bleach to 2.5 parts water
Sodium hypochlorite – liquid	5%	1 part bleach to 4 parts water
NaDCC (sodium dichloro-isocyanurate) powder	60%	17 grams to 1 litre water
NaDCC (1.5 g/ tablet) – tablets	60%	11 tablets to 1 litre water
Chloramine – powder	25%	80 g to 1 litre water
Bleaching powder	70%	7g g to 1 litre water
Any other	As per manufacturer's Instructions	

Annexure II - Disinfection Frequency and Sanitisation Guidelines

Area/Place	Disinfection Content	Disinfectant	Disinfection Method	Frequency
Work cell common surfaces	Including buttons, and other common surfaces	Hospital grade disinfectant or fresh 10% chlorine bleach solution (sodium hypochlorite solution), as appropriate	Spray with hand held sprayer or wipe	Minimum at the end of each shift
Offices, desk, and conference rooms	Table and chair surface		Spray with hand held sprayer or wipe	Minimum at the end of each shift
General objects often used or touched	Doors and windows, handles, faucets, sinks, and bathrooms		Spray with hand held sprayer or wipe	At least four times per day
Vending machines	Interface surfaces (pay, selection and vending surfaces)		Spray with sprayer	Daily
Transport vehicles	Common surfaces (e.g. seat surfaces rails, belts, door and window controls)		Spray with sprayer	After each use
All floors and walls	All general floors and walls at site		Mop	Periodic, where frequently touched; mop hard surfaces daily

Annexure III

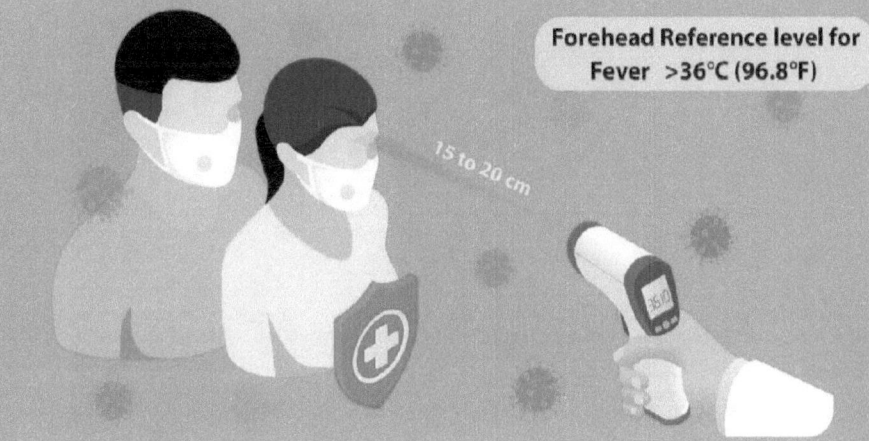

IR Thermometer Checks – Preventive controls

Why: Using the infrared thermometer to check the body's temperature requires a short amount of time without the risk of cross-infection. Therefore it's well-suited for use in places with a high flow of people.

Wear Mask and simple goggles/ glasses while carrying out this operation.

Forehead Reference level for Fever >36°C (96.8°F)

1. Hold Scanner at 15cm to 20cm distance. Scan across the forehead from center to left or right
2. If the Temperature reads
   - 36°C(96.8°F) and below then its Normal
   - 36.1 °C (97°F) or above – Indication of Fever
   - Recheck again to conclude
3. If its above 36.1 °C (97°F) - It could be normal fever or just high body temperature. For preventive measure ask/request employee /customer to avoid entry.

Comparison	Regular Thermometer		IR Thermometer		
Measurement Method	Tongue/ Rectum/ Armpit	Oral	Ear		Forehead
Accuracy	High	High	High		Low
Convenience and speed	Average	Average	High		Very high
Reference level for Fever	>37.5 °C (99.5°F)	>37.5°C(99.5°F)	>38°C(100.4°F)		>36°C(96.8°F)

Comparison among different measurement methods (www.mdk.gov.hk), Department of Health

Source: More Retail Limited

Annexure IV

Face Masks and its Important aspects

Type	Advantage	Duration	Filter level	Draw back
Cloth Mask	Washable	Can use whole day	80% of total atmospheric particle	Doesn't fit well. Allows air passage though gaps
Normal single layer PP Non-woven mask	Disposable	Breathing difficulty with prolonged use. More than 2 hours	Filters 90% of Atmospheric particle	Doesn't fit well. Allows air passage though gaps
3 ply mask (Non-woven)	Disposable	Breathing difficulty prolong use. More than 2 hours	Filters 90% of Atmospheric particle	Nose clip provision Fits well
P2.5 ,N95 mask	Usable as long as filter is not wet	Maximum 1 hour followed by normal breathing (without mask for an hour)	Filters 95% of 0.25 micron particles in the atmosphere	Breathing issue. Not recommended for Pregnant ladies and kids

Common issue with masks is that they typically have gaps between the face and the edges of the mask, that allows entrance of air and particles into the mask (and thus the user's respiratory system).Take care of following aspects while buying masks:

1. All mask must have a <u>Nose clip / adjustment provision</u> to hold fit at the nose
2. <u>Stretchable and adjustable loops or string tie</u> which enables compact fixing of the edges with face to avoid exposure to airborne particles in those gaps
3. Reuse cloth mask – Wash regularly with detergent and dry before using

Source: More Retail Limited

Annexure V

Source: World Health Organisation (WHO)

Annexure VI

Hand-washing technique with soap and water

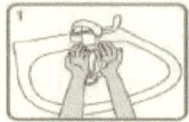
1. Wet hands with water

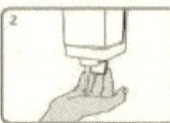
2. Apply enough soap to cover all hand surfaces

3. Rub hands palm to palm

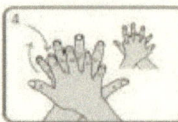
4. Rub back of each hand with palm of other hand with fingers interlaced

5. Rub palm to palm with fingers interlaced

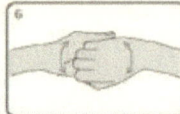
6. Rub with back of fingers to opposing palms with fingers interlocked

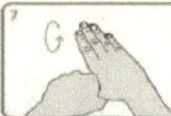
7. Rub each thumb clasped in opposite hand using a rotational movement

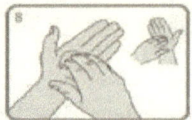
8. Rub tips of fingers in opposite palm in a circular motion

9. Rub each wrist with opposite hand

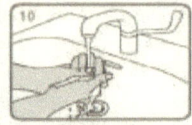
10. Rinse hands with water

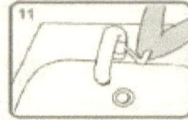
11. Use elbow to turn off tap

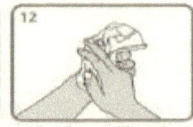
12. Dry thoroughly with a single-use towel

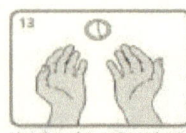
13. Hand washing should take 15–30 seconds

Annexure VII – Format for Self Declaration Form

COVID-19 Employee Self-Declaration Form

The safety of our employees remains the company's primary concern. To help prevent the spread of COVID-19 and reduce the potential risk of exposure to our employees we are conducting a simple screening questionnaire. Your participation is important to help us take precautionary measures to protect you and everyone in the building.

Thank you for your time and co-operation.

Contact Information

Name: Mobile No:

Email: Store Location:

Employee Details

Employee ID:

If the answer to question 1 below is yes, access to the store will be denied.

1. Are you showing any signs of one or more of the following symptoms? Temperature >38°C (100.4 °F) or higher, cough, shortness of breath, difficulty breathing, tiredness?

   ☐ YES   ☐ NO

2. Is the information you provided on this form true and correct to the best of your knowledge?

   ☐ YES

3. Did you come in contact with someone having COVID-19 symptoms during last 14 days?

   ☐ YES   ☐ NO

....
Signature

Overview

The COVID-19 has brought the entire world to its knees. It's an unknown enemy that over 200 countries across the globe are trying to protect its citizens from. According to the World Health Organization (WHO), COVID-19 spreads when people touch their eyes and nose after coming in contact with an infected person or contaminated surfaces or objects. Objects get contaminated when droplets from an infected person fall on them through coughing, sneezing or exhalation. It spreads in a manner similar to that of flu.

While, most persons infected with COVID-19 experience mild symptoms and recover, some require serious care. Risk of serious illness rises with age and weak immune system.

Social distancing seems to be the only way to control the spread of this virus. India has taken timely measures to contain the spread of the pandemic including imposing a lockdown.

Experts believe that the pandemic and the lockdown will forever change the way businesses function and consumers behave. Business will have to function while continuing the focus on health and safety of all involved.

Organisations that are prepared for the new reality with a complete SOP will reap the benefits. After re-opening manufacturing units, warehouses, stores and corporate offices post COVID-19 lockdown will be critical for all retail business units. They will have a difficult yet crucial task of ensuring safety and hygiene and instilling confidence in both internal and external customers in every possible way.

To help the Retail Business Units during this critical phase, Retailers Association of India set up a committee of experts represented by eminent members for putting together a set of guidelines for retail sector to follow. Members include –

1. Adhir Mane, CHRO - Lifestyle Business –Raymond

2. Chandrashekar Chavan, Chief Human Resources Officer - Apparel & Retail Business, Aditya Birla Group

3. G.R. Venkatesh, Chief Human Resource Officer - Reliance Retail Ltd

4. Priya Gopalakrishnan, Chief Human Resources Officer, Arvind Fashions Limited

5. Priya M Pillai, Head- HR, Retail & Corporate Functions - Titan Industries

6. Swetank Jain, Group Chief People Officer & Chief Communications Officer – Future Group

7. Seema Arora Nambiar, - Vice president - People Resource - Hardcastle Restaurants Pvt. Ltd.

8. Venkatramana B, President - Group HR - Landmark Group India

9. Venkatesh Raja, CHRO – Shoppers Stop Ltd

10. Kumar Rajagopalan, CEO, Retailers Association of India

11. Lawrence Fernandes, Director – Retail Learning & Membership

The objective of these guidelines is to provide a sound strategy for resuming businesses post COVID-19 lockdown. It also provides a framework for social distancing, right sanitization guidelines, workplace norms among others to ensure safety and hygiene for internal and external customers, which will remain of utmost importance.

> *Special thanks to the Indian Medical Association for helping Indian retail streamline operations in a safe and hygienic manner by rigorously reviewing the guidelines, improving them through their valuable inputs and approving them.*

Retailers operate in a variety of functions across the value chain. A typical Retail Value Chain looks like this:

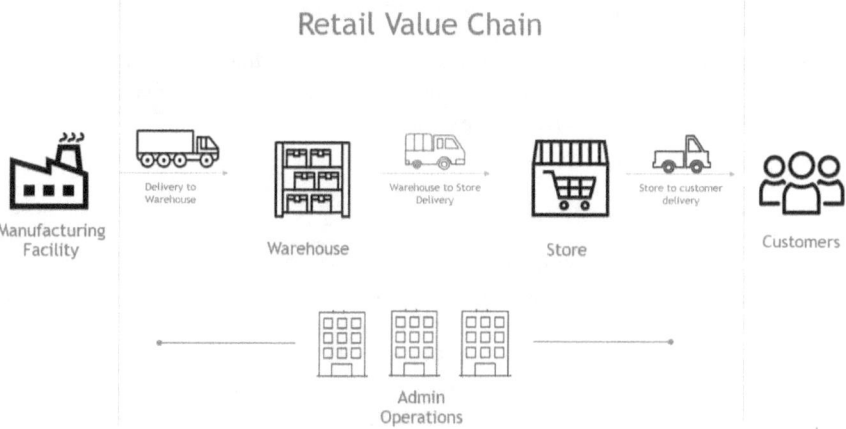

*This is a working document and will be frequently updated to reflect any new directives or recommended practices are introduced or implemented.

MANUFACTURING / WAREHOUSE OPERATIONS

Overall Precautionary Measures

- Provide Thermo-Guns and screen all personnel for fever and cold
- Provide masks to all employees (keep some masks in the spare in case an employee reports to work without a mask).
- Identify a room or area where someone who is feeling unwell or has symptoms can be safely isolated
- Create a Rapid Response Team of at least 2 managers who will monitor employees with infections / symptoms and will take necessary actions
- Empanel a doctor/doctors for health checks
- Get signed self-declarations **(Annexure-VII)** on health conditions by all personnel on a site

Social Distancing Measures

- Cancel all non-critical meetings, recreational activities, locker room access and mock drills
- Ensure that items required to be kept in lockers such as mobile phones should be sanitised before keeping them in and after they are retrieved
- Define maximum occupancy limit for all buildings and enclosed areas
- Increase employee transportation capacity and modes, ensure social distancing while transportation
- Cancel access of visitors to organisation's facilities/premises
- Restrict loading / unloading activities to ensure minimal interaction between personnel
- Space out employee amenities with markings on queue managers
- Stagger shift timings to ensure shifts do not over-lap so that social distancing is maintained at the start/end of shifts

Communication Measures

- Display approved signage across the facility mandating social distancing
- Display labour allocation information across multiple boards at prominent places across the building to avoid crowding
- Use Public Announcement (PA) systems for broadcasting messages reinforcing social distancing mandate
- Keep communicating and promoting the message that people need to stay at home even if they develop even mild symptoms of COVID-19

Sanitization Measures

- Establish protocols and processes for sanitization
- Sanitize all surfaces that are frequently touched at least once every 4 hours
- Ensure availability of Masks, Gloves for individuals engaged in processes where social distancing is not possible
- Ensure smaller shifts to limit exposure
- Put sanitizing hand rub dispensers at prominent places around the workplace. Make sure the dispensers are regularly refilled

DELIVERY / LOGISTICS OPERATIONS

- Tie-up with delivery partners for contactless delivery
- Ensure that company's delivery staff can visit the customer's residence with the products and requisite sanitization materials (mask, gloves, glasses and sanitizers)

Measures for Vendors

- Sanitize stocks when dispatched from warehouse and re-sanitize when accepted at store
- Screen all drivers (temperature check). Also ensure they wear masks and sanitize hands
- Making sure that drivers and loading-unloading staff have access to places where they can wash their hands with soap and water

STORE OPERATIONS

Overall Precautionary Measures

- Provide thermo-guns to screen all personnel for fever and Cold
- Get signed self-declarations **(Annexure-VII)** on health conditions by all personnel on a site
- Identify a room or area where someone who is feeling unwell or has symptoms can be safely isolated
- Create a Rapid Response Team of at least 2 managers who will monitor employees with infections / symptoms and will take necessary actions
- Install no-touch trash bins, instruments such as sneeze guards / protective screens at checkouts/cash counters
- Plan store openings keeping COVID-19 hotspots and non-hotspot areas in mind
  - Opening of stores in COVID-19 hotspots can be delayed. However, the stores in non-hotspots can open post lockdown
- Encourage employees to use their private vehicles while commuting to work. Consider providing fuel allowance
- Encourage quick shopping options like order on phone and pick from outside the store

Ventilation

Ensure that the stores and retail outlets are well ventilated with proper air circulation. Avoid using air conditioners without fresh air intake. In case, that is not possible, follow a mix of the below principles depending on the place and options available.

General guiding principles
- Set the temperature all air conditioning devices in the range of 24-30° c.
- Ensure relative humidity is in the range of 40-70%
- Ensure maximum intake of fresh air by opening of doors and or windows of the store several times during the day.
- Avoid recirculation of air to the extent possible
- Ensure adequate cross ventilation
- Use exhaust fans to facilitate replacement of air by
- Frequently clean and sanitise filters of indoor cooling units to ensure air sanitization
- Ensure that there is no direct contact of air.

Social distancing Measures

- Make floor markings at the tills to ensure social distancing
- Set up prioritized shopping hours for instance one hour every Monday, Wednesday and Friday morning for vulnerable and elderly customers and frontline workers
- Manage stores with minimum number of staff with staggered days as footfall may not be high even after lifting of the lockdown
- Introduce disposable token system to avoid crowding at stores
- Define the maximum customer occupancy inside a store basis the size of the store to ensure a distance of 6 feet between customers and limit contact while queuing

Sanitization Measures

- Install sanitization products, and preventive guideline posters at all entry and exit points
- Disinfect surfaces, including doorknobs, handrails, the POS system, tables and desks, front entrance, carts, registers and bathrooms with 1% sodium hypochlorite or phenolic disinfectants at regular intervals for the entire duration a store is open. The guidelines for preparing fresh 1% sodium hypochlorite solution is at **Annexure I**
- Frequent sanitisation of store premises at regular intervals to be carried out. Disinfection frequency and sanitisation guidelines can be found in **Annexure II**
- Provide Bio-Degradable gloves, masks to staff

- Place sanitizing hand rub dispensers at prominent places around the workplace Make sure these dispensers are regularly refilled
- Ensure physical distancing by keeping a distance of at least 6 feet between employees
- Mandate the staff using public transport to sanitize themselves before entering the store
- Encourage customers to use cleaning stations to wipe trolleys, basket, etc.
- Ensure that items required to be kept in lockers such as mobile phones should be sanitised before keeping them in and after they are retrieved

Display, Merchandizing and Sampling

- Food & Grocery:
    - Pre-pack loose commodities to avoid contamination
    - Limit number of employees handling food items
    - Ensure close surveillance of employees handling food items for possible infections
    - Ensure all employees sanitize themselves before handling food items
    - Ensure adequate staffing in all sections especially those selling loose products and Fruits & Vegetables
    - Ensure employees assist customers in packing and picking the products
- Non-Food:
    - Ensure trial rooms are disinfected with spray, pre and post each customer trial to build customer confidence and for staff safety
    - Request customers to wait for 5 minutes to iron clothes, wherever possible, with availability of steam iron before packing, so that the product is free of contaminants
    - Ensure no customer or staff touches merchandise without proper sanitization
    - Encourage customers to only touch what they intend to purchase
    - Set up a process wherein tried garments are kept in dedicated trial rooms. Next morning, the garments from the previous day are to be steamed and put back on display
    - Set up a process wherein hangers are retrieved and kept in a separate carton marked 'TO BE SANITIZED' in the trial room aisle area. These hangers to be sanitized before reuse
    - Ensure trial room tokens are sanitized after every use
    - Restrict the number of items that can be exchanged / returned for online orders. Furthermore, set up proper procedure so that returns are thoroughly sanitized

Customer Sales

- Billing & Payment process
    - Encourage contactless payment options such as Paytm, Google Pay, UPI

- o Mandate cashiers to extend a tray to receive or return currency / cards for payments
- o Ensure plenty of cash tills and mobile checkouts to reduce billing time
- o Adopt measures to sanitize cash before it gets accepted
- o Ensure cashiers wear gloves while dispensing cash
- o Replace physical bills with softcopy to be sent to customers via email / SMS
- o Allow customers to exit the store if there is no beep. Do away with bill punching / checking of carry bags post purchase
- o Direct customers to collect sanitised shopping bags from bag holder

- Billing & Other Staff
  - o Make it mandatory for shop staff to wear face masks. Dispense with handshakes, use a non-contact method for greetings
  - o Make it compulsory for employees to wash their hands when they arrive and every time they enter the premises, as well as frequently throughout the day

ADMIN / CENTRALIZED OPERATIONS

Overall Precautionary Measures

- Provide thermo-guns to screen all personnel for fever and Cold
- Get signed self-declarations **(Annexure-VII)** on health conditions by all personnel on a site
- Identify a room or area where someone who is feeling unwell or has symptoms can be safely isolated
- Create a Rapid Response Team of at least 2 managers who will monitor employees with infections / symptoms and will take necessary actions
- Conduct daily fever checks—Every individual to be checked for the body temperature through infrared thermometers without fail
- Make sanitizers available at all entry and exit points
- Defer joining of employees traveling using public transports such as train/bus/taxis/auto in the initial stages. Instruct employees commuting by their own vehicles to avoid using drivers

Social Distancing norms

- Define maximum occupancy for all buildings and enclosed areas
- Restrict gathering in groups; avoid any kind of meeting of more than 2-3 persons at a time
- Mandate employees to have lunch at their own work stations; no employee to be allowed to wash their lunch box in the wash basin

- Limit number of employees using washrooms at the same time to 2 people, forbid queuing at the entrance
    - Sanitary workers must use separate set of cleaning equipment for toilets (mops, nylon scrubber) and separate set for sink and commode). They should always wear disposable protective gloves while cleaning a toilet.
    - 70% Alcohol solution can be used to wipe down surfaces where the use of bleach is not suitable, e.g. metal. (Chloroxylenol (4.5-5.5%)/ Benzalkonium Chloride or any other disinfectants found to be effective against coronavirus may be used as per manufacturer's instructions)
    - Always use freshly prepared 1% sodium hypochlorite.
    - Do not use disinfectants spray on potentially highly contaminated areas (such as toilet bowl or surrounding surfaces) as it may create splashes which can further spread the virus.
    - To prevent cross contamination, discard cleaning material made of cloth (mop and wiping cloth) in appropriate bags after cleaning and disinfecting. Wear new pair of gloves and fasten the bag.
    - Disinfect all cleaning equipment after use and before using in other area
    - Disinfect buckets by soaking in bleach solution or rinse in hot water

Employee Working Cadence

- Cancel all non-critical meetings, recreational activities and corporate events
- Encourage remote working for as long as possible (Functions and Roles that can work effectively from home should be continued to Work From Home)
- Conduct virtual meetings using online apps/platforms (Skype, Zoom, Webex)
- Ensure that not more than 50% staff works from office
- Stagger shifts as much as possible to avoid over-lap
- In a meeting/conference/office room, if someone is coughing, without following respiratory etiquettes or mask, the areas around his/her seat should be vacated and cleaned with 1% sodium hypochlorite.

Employee Communication

- Put up signs and posters around the workplace to remind workers and others of the risks of COVID-19 and measures necessary to stop its spread
- Encourage employees to wash their hands with soap for 20 seconds before and after using wash rooms
- Provide all employees with training on preventing transmission of COVID-19, including initial and routine/refresher training
- Ensure frequent communication using WhatsApp and other communication tools
- Display posters promoting respiratory hygiene. Combine this with other communication measures such as guidance from occupational health and safety officers, briefing at meetings and information on intranet

www.ingramcontent.com/pod-product-compliance
Lightning Source LLC
Chambersburg PA
CBHW030936180526
45163CB00002B/590